Cover design & layout: Wet Frog Studios

ISBN 978-1-512-27862-0

I dedicate this book to all the women in my life who have been a part of my journey. I wouldn't be the woman I am today with out all of you, and for that I am grateful.

Chasing Pigeons

A MEMOIR OF ONE
WOMAN'S JOURNEY
OF HEALING

Jennifer Mahnke

INTRODUCTION

There is a picture of myself from when I was about four years old that has always fascinated me.

Even haunted me.

I am chasing pigeons in Paris outside The Louvre. It isn't anything special in and of itself. Just the classic picture of a little girl in mid 70's polyester clothing running in a patch of grass. You can't even see the pigeons.

It's the carefree, joyful girl that I have always found so fascinating. For most of my life I had no idea who that girl was. I couldn't relate to her, her attitude, her outlook. And I was jealous that she could be that way and I could not. So, perhaps the most frustrating thing was the knowledge that the girl was me. I was that girl, but I had no idea why I could not live like she clearly was: free, joyful and full of life.

What happened between the taking of that picture and the rest of my life? What took away that joy, that freedom? More importantly, would I ever get it back and if so, what would it take to get to that place? It seemed impossible and I used to live as one destined to never know.

Bad things happened in my life, some not too long after the picture in Paris was taken. I do not want to dwell on the specifics of those things, but the general experience needs to be mentioned in order to move on with the telling of my story. When I was about five or six I was sexually abused by an extended member of my family. Sexual abuse is horrible no matter when or how it happens in the life of a person, but when it happens at such an early age it can profoundly interrupt and confuse the person's growth in understanding who they are, their value, and their purpose. It changes outlooks, perspectives of others and the ability to trust. It also leaves you with intense feelings of shame. Deep shame.

Sexual abuse has varying effects upon people: some try to deal with the experience by delving into other sexual experiences while others clam up and have difficulty relating to others on any level. While I didn't tend toward either extreme, I did enter into a pattern of relating to men that would cause me years of frustration, sadness and self-hatred.

I was looking for someone to come along and make me whole.

To fill all the hurting and empty places inside of me.

So I placed inappropriate hopes upon each guy I met. And the pattern was always the same. I would be attracted to him. I would flirt, and perhaps he would too. I would get high hopes and plan our future out in my mind. Then all my attention would turn him off and drive him away leaving me empty, feeling stupid and lonely.

I did have a few boyfriends though. My first was in college and that one did a number on me. We were both messed up people. It ended up being an emotionally abusive relationship for me, further adding to all the issues I had with myself and relating to men. It was the classic I Can Fix This Guy and We'll Live Happily Ever After scenario. I know he loved me and cared for me. But I felt like I was kept at the end of a tether. He couldn't handle being in a committed, responsible relationship with me, but he didn't want me to be with anyone else either. He'd let me go away just far enough and then yank me back in long enough to keep me connected to him. It was a mess.

I was a mess.

Well, toward the end of my twenties, all this had taken its toll on me. By that time I was sincerely convinced that there must be something wrong with me since no one wanted to be with me. I knew it wasn't my appearance. I'm an attractive woman. Men had always made that clear to me. That left the inside of me. The part of me that would always be me. I was watching my body start to age a little and knew I must be doomed to singleness. Who would want me after the outside fell apart since there was something wrong with me on the inside?

How broken my life's events and experiences had left me.

And in my brokenness I became more broken as I believed the lies I heard the world telling me about who I was. There was a deep anguish in my innermost self. A chasm I was falling into with no visible way out.

I wrote the following paragraphs one day in the midst of a time of struggle with myself and life:

> *The woman awoke and found herself on the shores of a deep blue ocean. The sunlight danced on the water in a million different sparkles. A lone bird soared high upon the wind, so high that she only felt the slightest breeze on her bare arms. The gentle waves were the only break to the quiet of the morning. Peace. Perfect peace was the only thing she felt upon awakening. The woman reveled in that perfect peace for a while.*
>
> *As sleep slowly left her being, she began to really look at her surroundings. The closer she looked, the more damage and wreckage she noticed. It seemed to be rising from the ground around her. Split second glimpses of sad, empty scenes from her past flashed before her mind and she was reminded of where she'd come from. She cried out to the morning. She wanted to push away the pain and damage around her. Where was the peace she saw just a few minutes earlier?*

Like that woman, I knew that life had been created good. And there were times when it all appeared to be at peace, either as a façade on the outside, or within me. But then I would remember. Someone or something would come along and remind me that I was alone, broken, forgotten.

That life was unfair.

Another friend would get married.

The girl who seemed to have it all would indeed get it all!

Or I would be home alone again on a Friday night while everyone else was out having fun.

The cute guy I just met would spend his evening talking with someone else and not me.

My clothes would not fit me one day and I would hate my body, wishing I could look more like the perfect women in the magazines. The list could go on. The bottom line was that life was not fair and I had an empty pit that threatened to consume me with loneliness, bitterness, shame, and sadness.

However, at the same time that I knew all of these things, I also knew that more was possible. Life didn't have to stay the way it was. Healing and growth were possible somehow. The day after I wrote the above paragraphs I wrote this one:

> *Slowly, her surroundings began to change again. They changed, and yet she couldn't quite figure out how. It gradually dawned on her! The waves! The gentle, persistent waves were wearing down the damage around her. Where there once were sharp, jagged edges, there were now smooth surfaces. Before long, the last of the damage that had broken her peace was washed away with one big cleansing wave. Peace once again filled the beach and her very being as her heart reveled in a glorious new day.*

There was a hope in me for something more. A whole life that wasn't dictated by the wreckage of past pain and lies. The peace that is beyond understanding. I yearned for that in my life and that yearning became like a prayer within me to be that little girl in Paris that I had once been.

I think this hope exists in all of us, even if it is only a flicker of an idea that one barely dares to dream of. Sometimes that flicker may become a flame for a while. Sometimes it starts to go out again. And at other times it is only something another person can hope in for us.

I do not know the circumstances of your life. Perhaps you can relate very well to my story. Maybe it sounds familiar, but yours has its own twists and turns. Or maybe your life has completely different experiences, but the results of those things have left you in the same lonely, broken place. And just maybe your life has been without deep times of hurt, but you know people who deeply struggle and you hurt for them.

No matter who you are or what you have gone through in life we all have hurts, disappointments, brokenness; no matter the degree of these experiences we all know the effects of them.

None of us are exempt from pain.

From the need for deep healing and restoration.

From the need for the cleansing waves of peace to wash over us.

How does this healing and cleansing happen? We can want it with all our might, but how does it actually take place? How can we take the wreckage of a broken life and make it whole, give it purpose and value and live a vibrant life of joy?

How do we become the little girl chasing pigeons in Paris?

I do not claim to have all the answers, but I do know my own experience of healing. I have lived a journey of becoming the little girl again. It wasn't easy or fun, but I can now say that I know that little girl in the picture. I can relate to her joy, her freedom and her love of life. I know what brought me to this place and I want to share that story with you knowing that maybe something might inspire you to take this journey too. Knowing that we do not have to continue living with the shame and hurt. Knowing that true redemption, freedom and peace is possible in this life! I believe my story is the story of all women and I cannot keep it to myself.

Let your journey intersect with mine for this time and see where it leads you. Perhaps the little girl within you will chase pigeons with joyful abandon again too!

CHAPTER ONE
An Anchor in the Waves

There are many threads interwoven into the story of my life: my relationship with Jesus, my time in the country of England, music, prayer, and the ocean. All of these things have a prominent place in my life, my desires, my focus, my interests. So, I start my story sitting on a damp grassy patch of land in Tintagel, England with a misty rain coming down upon me as I stare out at the raging ocean waves…

In the late 90's, my family took a vacation in England for two weeks and this one afternoon found us at the remains of the castle where legend says King Arthur was born. The land, like the day, was raw and isolating. The wind and rain kept me from taking the precarious trip with my family across a narrow walkway to an island that was part of the fortress. And I longed for some time to myself. I wandered around among the ruins and then settled myself down to watch the waves.

As usually happens when I am alone, and at the ocean, I began talking with God.

I do not remember exactly what I was thinking that day, but I do know it was a time of searching and yearning. Searching for who I am and what I was to do with my life. Yearning for more out of life, more of what I knew I was missing even if I could not put a name to it. My heart was crying out for something more than I knew or had. I was filled with such longing for fuller life and purpose that I felt the intensity of it in the pit of my stomach.

I felt lost, alone, small and utterly out of control.

Then God opened my eyes to what was right in front of me: the waves.

The massive, powerful waves.

The grey water was swelling up and crashing into a little rock-covered cove about three stories down from where I sat. There was nothing peaceful or calming about the ocean that day; it was all wild, sharp and rough.

I started contemplating the waves and saw that there is nothing in this world that can control them. We might be able to construct walls to keep them from us, but they remain. They are a force, raw and untamed. My thoughts moved on from there to consider that the waves are always there. We can always count on the waves because the tide constantly comes in and out. They are consistent and predictable.

As I thought about these truths of the ocean I realized that God is the same as the waves: wild and raw while constantly present. And this brought me great comfort. As small and unsure as I felt, I knew then that I was not alone. There is a great and powerful God who is also there with me who will always be. Like the waves constantly coming to shore I can count on God to always be present in my life, my experiences and my future.

Why do I begin with this story, besides the fact that it is chronologically toward the beginning?

Because without this experience and the realizations that came with it, I could not have made it through some of the other things to come. I can not tell you how many times I have gone back in my mind to that half hour or so on the edge of England looking out at the waves. Remembering that God is raw and all-powerful while at the same time ever present and constant has provided me the strength, courage and permission to keep going. It has given me incredible peace in the midst of raging emotion and turmoil to remember that God is more powerful and stronger than what I was going through at any given time.

God speaks to us, reveals himself to us in so many different times and ways. It is important to mark them in our minds and hearts so we can lean on them when things get tough, lonely, frightening and out of control. I wrote about it in my journal and have drawn and painted it many times. The image is always with me, along with the truths it represents.

God is bigger than the lies I believed that said I was insignificant, damaged, unwanted and of little value.

He is more powerful than the hold my abuse had upon me was.

More powerful than the fear and distrust that held me back from good relationships and experiences.

He is more constant than the best of friends.

More consistent in love, grace and acceptance and always available to listen, even in the middle of the night when I desperately need someone.

The experience of the waves has served as an anchor in the storm you could say. And I am so thankful.

Chapter One:
Personal Application

EXERCISE 1

Find a quiet place to sit where you will not be disturbed by the world around you. Think about your life and experiences you have had that stand out as significant. Is there a place, time or experience that you find yourself thinking about that holds a sense of peace, power or special application to your life? One that feels like standing on firm ground? That you go back to again and again in times of trouble or doubt?

It may take time to find this anchor for your life, but give it time. For some, several times or places may stand out as significant and that is good too. Once you have something in mind, write down the experience getting down as much detail as possible. What time of day was it? What was the weather like? Do you remember the smells in the air? What feelings were going on inside of you? Who else was around?

Then, consider what it is about this time, place or experience that makes it a foundation for your life. What is it that brings peace or meaning? What was, and is, God wanting to communicate to you about himself? Yourself? Your life at the time and your life now? Having an understanding about this experience in your life will allow it to be more than just that experience. It will help transform it into the anchor that you are needing in your life as you face doubts, questions and pains. As you struggle with who you are and who you are becoming. Take time to pray, meditate and journal about what you are thinking and feeling.

EXERCISE 2

If you are a writer, take what you have written, thought of and discovered about your anchor experience and write a narrative of it, giving the whole thing flesh and blood. Write it out in such a way that if someone else were to read it they would feel like they are there. Not that another has to read it, but this exercise will help your anchor to become as real to you today, and in the future when you need to recall it, as when you first experienced it.

EXERCISE 3

If you are artistic, paint, draw, collage or use your medium of choice to depict your anchor and all it means to you. Having a visual reminder of your anchor will be an incredible help in remembering just why it is an anchor. Having it around you in your everyday life could have incredible value as you work through your past pains and your present self.

EXERCISE 4

If you are a verbal processor, find someone you trust and talk through these questions with them. Or, use a tape recorder and talk through the questions on your own. This way you can transcribe your talking or just have it to listen to.

CHAPTER TWO
Me and Missions

There are two things that I used to always tell God that I did not want: I did not want to be a missionary and I did not want to marry a pastor. So, I have to laugh because not only did God lead me to do missions work in England (and I loved it!), but I am married to a man who has his Masters of Divinity and has been a pastor! I believe God has a sense of humor, but I also believe that I was fighting that which I was afraid of.

And I am glad God won.

Not long after my trip to England with my family, I felt God challenging me in my resolve to never be a missionary. I was living in Chicago at the time and was active at my church there. I was asked to find people to share their experiences or thoughts on missionary work in five to ten minute slots of time during the church service. I joked with someone that I hoped this wasn't God's plan to get me to share anything in front of the church and was working to make sure that didn't happen. But someone did cancel on me last minute and I could not find anyone else to take his place. And God had been working in me, in my thoughts and conversations with people, and I knew I had something to share about the topic of "Me and Missions".

What I had come to realize, and what I shared that morning, is that I am just me, and God is God of the universe. Who was I to tell God I would not go to another country and do work for him if that is how he wants to use me to touch the lives of other people and share Jesus with them? After all, just like the waves, I knew God was powerful and constant and I could trust in him to be that for me no matter where I was.

Even if I was a missionary.

I then actually got really excited about the idea of doing missionary work and started looking into it. I found a few good organizations and sent for information on them, particularly from those at work in England since that is a country I dearly love. Nothing happened though and I just continued living in Chicago. But I knew missionary work was still something God was leading me toward, and that when the time was right, I would know and that I would go.

It happened almost two years later.

And I can still picture it all so clearly. I came home from work one night in mid January. I came in my backdoor into the kitchen. The light was on over the stove, casting a warm glow over the room. I went to the front door, checked my mail and carried it back with me into the kitchen to sort it at the counter. There was a newsletter from the organization Youth With A Mission (YWAM) toward the back. I glanced through it and set it down. Almost immediately I picked it back up and looked at it again. And then I found that I could not put it down.

Something was compelling me to keep it in my hand. I wasn't reading it, just staring at it. And I knew that now was the time for me to go. I can't explain it any other way. All I could do was look at the newsletter and know it was time for me to go be a missionary in England.

I spent the next two weeks in denial, but eventually I filled out the application to go. A month after that, I found out that I had been accepted to be a part of a Discipleship Training School (DTS) at a mission base south of London. And a month after that, I was all packed up to move my things back home to Massachusetts and to leave from there for England.

Little did I realize it then, but that summer in England, and the one following, were to be the most pivotal summers in my life and are the center of my story of healing.

Chapter Two:
Personal Application

EXERCISE 1

Look back over your life; what are the significant events that stand out in your mind as pivotal or defining? Going away to school, moving to a new town, a new job, a relationship, a new beginning or something ending? Which of these marks a significant change in your life and the direction you were heading in? Understanding where you have been and changes you have made can help bring understanding and perspective for the present and the future.

EXERCISE 2

For further thought about the significant events of your life, take time to journal about those that really stand out as most defining. Who was involved? What were your feelings then, and now, about that time? How did that event bring change to your life? How has it contributed to who you are right now?

EXERCISE 3

If you are a visual person, create a timeline of your life, filling in the events that stand out to you as defining or significant. Use this to consider how these events have given you direction, or how they can speak to you now about the direction you need to head in. Are you going where you see God leading you? What changes might you need to make in your thoughts, attitudes, job, course of study or your goals to go in that direction?

CHAPTER THREE
Singing in the Toilets

Moving to England was quite a shock to my system. It wasn't so much being in another country, because I'd been there a few times and even lived there for a year as a child. The shock had more to do with the drastic change in my circumstances of living. In Chicago I'd been living alone in my own apartment, working for the deans at the university I had attended and enjoying life with a solid group of friends. Then all of a sudden I found myself living in a large manor house in the middle of the English countryside with a group of eleven other people from six different countries and sharing a room with five other women.

Oh, and instead of sleeping in my fairly new queen sized bed, I was the occupant of the bottom bunk of a three-tiered bunk bed!

Life had definitely taken an interesting turn.

As much as I initially fought being there, and the desire to turn and run home, I quickly knew that this would be a powerful time in my life. I heard people many times talk about how time at a DTS is like living in a green house for a plant. The plant is there in the warm, protected environment that enables it to grow quickly and freely. A DTS is a green house for people. We were taken out of our "normal" lives for a time and given the time, space, permission and nurture we needed to face issues, to struggle with ideas, and life, and to learn. We were given opportunities for a variety of experiences in ministry that we might never get at home.

For those who are not familiar with YWAM or a DTS I need to briefly explain. YWAM is the largest missions organization in the world. It has bases all over that are centers for giving people an initial experience of missionary work and a more permanent home for those doing long term work in that specific area.

If you want to get involved with YWAM you have to first go through one of their Discipleship Training Schools. They take people of a variety of ages, though mostly those out of high school or college and into their twenties, and give them a first missions experience. Each school begins with a lecture phase. People are brought in from all over the world to teach on a variety of topics for anywhere from a day up to a week at a time. Topics like the nature and character of God; destiny; prayer; sin, repentance and restitution; relationships; and yes, missions. Then the group of students is sent somewhere for the outreach phase, usually another country, to get involved in all sorts of ministries, often times as a support to the long term missionaries working there. In this way, people are given the chance to see if missionary work, or formal ministry in general, is something they want to pursue, as well as just growing in who they are as Christians in a world of need.

One aspect of living in a large house with 25 to 45 other people is that the work of keeping the house clean has to be taken on by everyone, everyday. We had rotations for cleaning up dinner dishes and one other work duty assigned to us to do Monday through Friday. I cleaned the toilets with my friend Simon from Switzerland. Now, to say that I cleaned "toilets" in England also means that we cleaned the sinks and showers and any other surface found in a "bathroom". I offered to be a part of that work duty team because I thought no one else would want to do it and it ended up being the top choice for a number of us!

Who knew that cleaning the toilets could be such a wonderful and meaningful experience, but it was.

We would start on the third floor in the guy's toilet room and shower room, go down to the second floor for the girls full bath and a second guy's shower room and finish off on the main floor with a men's and a women's toilet. It usually took us about an hour and a half every day and was something that I usually didn't want to do when it was time, but was so glad to have done once we had.

What, you may ask, was so wonderful about cleaning toilets?

There are a couple of things that come to mind. It really is a humbling experience to clean toilets everyday for you and your friends. You see the dirty side of life when cleaning a toilet or shower drain. But it is such an act of service for others and I found value in this.

The most amazing, and perhaps unexpected, thing about cleaning the toilets was the joy we both experienced doing it.

Joy? In cleaning toilets? How is that possible?

Well, it is when you sing your way through the job. Simon and I very quickly began singing our way through our work. I'm not sure how it started, but we couldn't go through a day of cleaning without song. We learned which bathrooms made which songs sound the best, our favorite being the men's shower on the second floor. It had tile on all the surfaces and the notes and words had a way of floating around us. Sometimes we would get there and just stand and sing for a while before working. We'd also save specific songs for that bathroom. Simon could sing harmony and I have to say we sounded pretty amazing at times.

It is an odd thing to be singing praise to our God in the middle of a bathroom, but I experienced some of the best worship in that way.

And it lifted our spirits and those of the people who heard us. The best thing was to start our day cleaning on the top floor with a song, go through all the bathrooms and make it to the basement to put our used rags in the wash only to hear someone who had been cleaning in the basement the entire time singing the same song we had started with an hour and a half ago and three floors up! Songs would make their way through the house. Maria would hear us first as she was vacuuming the stairs and so begin singing. Someone else would hear her and join in only to pass it along to another. Joy would descend upon the house as we all went about our work duties.

My time cleaning and singing with Simon is another of those anchors that has held me fast. Having joy in our lives is not dependent upon us being happy, or in good circumstances. The world can be crashing down around us and we can have joy in our hearts. It is a matter of what your focus is within your heart. If we focus and dwell on the horrible or painful things of life, then that is what will come out of us.

But when we center ourselves on God, on singing songs of praise, love and the truth of God, then that is what comes out of us no matter what our outward experiences are.

Does this mean that we should never think about life's difficulties and pains? No, we have to in order to gain understanding, perspective, healing and growth. However, we can still have joy while doing those things. Perhaps this is a hard or incomprehensible thing to believe possible, but that is partly why I am telling my story. I could not have made it through various times and experiences without this joy. It is not something we can manufacture, but something God freely gives us when we turn our hearts and focus upon him. He gives His joy to us so that we can know it in all situations. It is one of the fruits of the spirit the Bible talks about; the fruit of a person turning their life over to God in love and worship. This freely given joy was an anchor. It still is an anchor.

Song, singing, giving praise to God is an anchor in my life.

Actually, in many ways it is more like a kite in my life. When I sing my spirit soars like a kite caught on a wind high up in the blue sky. And it dances up there, enjoys the view. Because God fills me with joy.

That same summer that Simon and I sang our way through the bathrooms, a group of people came to stay for a few days at the YWAM base I was at. They came to share their story with us and to minister to us in their unique way. They were a punk-rock band that were loud and a lot of fun. But the next morning they were just a group of ordinary people who sat with us and prayed with us.

We were together in small groups and a member of the band was with each group. We took turns praying for each person individually and writing down the things that people said. While I was being prayed for the woman from the band in our group said she saw a picture of a bird in a cage. When the bird began to sing the cage would open up and the bird could fly away. She said that when I am feeling like that bird in the cage all I have to do is start singing and the bars will fall away and I'll be free to fly off. That imagery, and the truth it represents, has helped me so many times while in the midst of tears, struggle and pain.

When we are dealing with all the crap that life throws at us we can indeed feel trapped, unable to move. Either because we are so confused about where to go, or because some things in life have a paralyzing effect upon us. Whatever the reason, we can feel locked in a cage with no way out.

Song, and singing in particular, has become my "way out".

Once I turn my focus upon God, singing about his goodness, his love, his character, what he has done for me in freeing me from my sin and brokenness, his joy comes rushing in and I become that bird that is able to fly away. Not to fly away to avoid dealing with whatever is before me, but away from the fear, the shame, the self doubt and hatred that keep me from being able to move forward in and through the pain.

This is powerful and essential in dealing with our hurts and struggles. We have to be free to move forward. To no longer believe the lies that hold us back. To be able to forgive those who have hurt us so we can move on. So we can no longer give in to those defense mechanisms that were necessary in the moment of abuse, but that are hurtful to us and to others now.

The chorus of one of my favorite worship songs says:

> *In the spirit, he is real*
> *In the spirit, I can feel*
> *In the spirit, I am healed*
> *By the power of his love*
> *In the spirit, I'm alive*
> *In the spirit, I can fly*
> *In the spirit of the living God…*
> ("In the Spirit" by Don Potter. EagleStar Productions, 1998.)

Through song I can receive all that God has to give me so that I can live through and move beyond all the pain and difficulty of life.

In song I come to life.

I find freedom.

And I know joy.

Chapter Three:
Personal Application

EXERCISE 1

Consider when you have known joy in your life. What were the circumstances? Has it been brief or consistent? Hard to come by or easy? Do you know it in all circumstances or in just some? The Bible says that we can know joy in all circumstances, the good and the bad. The easy and the difficult. Do you believe this? Would you like to believe this? Do you embrace this truth whole-heartedly or does it scare you? Read over and reflect on the following verses that speak about joy. Ask God to open your heart to what he wants to teach you about his joy in your life in all circumstances. Write out, or share with someone, what you hear God telling you. Ask God to help you believe and live the things he reveals to you.

> Habakkuk 3:17-18 — *"Though the fig tree does not bud and there are no grapes on the vines, though the olive crop fails and the fields produce no food, though there are no sheep in the pen and no cattle in the stalls, yet I will rejoice in The Lord, I will be joyful in God my Savior."*

> John 15:9-11 — *"As the Father has loved me, so have I loved you. Now remain in my love. If you obey my commands, you will remain in my love, just as I have obeyed my Father's commands and remain in his love. I have told you this so that my joy may be in you and that your joy may be complete."*

Galatians 5:22-25 — *"But the fruit of the Spirit is love, joy, peace, patience, kindness, goodness, faithfulness, gentleness and self-control. Against such things there is no law. Those who belong to Christ Jesus have crucified the sinful nature with its passions and desires. Since we live by the Spirit, let us keep in step with the Spirit."*

Ephesians 5:19-20 — *"Speak to one another with psalms, hymns and spiritual songs. Sing and make music in your heart to The Lord, always giving thanks to God the Father for everything, in the name of our Lord Jesus Christ."*

Philippians 4:4 — *"Rejoice in The Lord always. I will say it again: Rejoice!"*

1 Thessalonians 5:16 — *"Be joyful always."*

Look up the words joy, joyful or anything along those lines in the concordance of your Bible and read the verses you find.

EXERCISE 2
What songs have touched you? Spoken to your heart? Write them out to have around you. Put them in your day planner, on your bathroom mirror or refrigerator door. Put it on your desk at work or anywhere you will see it repeatedly. Put them on your iPod and listen to them while driving, exercising, doing the dishes. If you are an artist create a visual rendering of the song with or without words.

EXERCISE 3
If songs do not speak to you in the same way, what does? Where do you find joy? Think back on your life to times

of joy; what was the vehicle for God's joy in those times and circumstances? A time of serving others? A verse or verses from the Bible? An experience of meditating on scripture? Hearing another person's words of truth or wisdom? A specific life experience? Some aspect of nature or time spent in it? Or something else? Write, draw, talk, or think on what comes to mind. How can you draw on this vehicle, song or scripture in the present? Is there a pattern you can see in your life of joy coming from the same or similar things that you can learn from and draw upon in your present circumstances?

EXERCISE 4

How are you trying to avoid or cover over pain and brokenness to feel better instead of allowing God to fill you with his joy in the midst of your pain? Spend some time alone with God, take a long walk, get up early when all is quiet. Ask him to open your eyes as to how you might be avoiding issues in an attempt to feel better instead of allowing God's joy to fill you as you live in the midst of your issues, difficult situation or brokenness.

EXERCISE 5

Henri Nouwen wrote, "Jesus shows, both in his teachings and in his life, that true joy often is hidden in the midst of our sorrow, and that the dance of life finds its beginnings in grief. He says, *'Unless the grain of wheat dies, it cannot bear fruit...Unless we lose our lives, we cannot find them; unless the Son of Man dies, he cannot send the Spirit.'*" (Here and Now, p 42-43. The Crossroad Publishing Company, New York; 1994) Consider this statement. What is Nouwen saying and how does this effect how you view your situation? Can you see the joy in the midst of your grief? If not, ask God to open your eyes to see it.

CHAPTER FOUR
A Burden Lifted

God didn't waste any time in bringing me to confront issues in my life. The first summer I was in England was all about me letting go and healing from the relationship I'd had during college. The emotionally abusive relationship.

The second week of the DTS we had a speaker come to talk with us for a whole week about sin, repentance and restitution. It didn't take long for a specific incident from my college relationship to begin weighing very heavily upon me. At that point in life I had gotten over him. I was no longer in love with him. I no longer wanted him back. I had come to recognize the negative aspects of our relationship and how they had effected me. But there was this one thing left to deal with and it was something so hard and hurtful that I thought I would never be rid of it.

I believed that I would carry this one around with me for the rest of my life.

But God had other ideas.

Spring semester of my Junior year in college, my on-again-off-again boyfriend went abroad to study for the semester. That semester was probably my best one during college. He wasn't there to inflict the I Don't Want You But I Don't Want Anyone Else To Have You Either messages and behaviors on me. So it was a time of growth and healing. And learning to trust in God. I truly did try to move on from that relationship and at some point decided that when he got back I would tell him that I only wanted to be friends with him.

That summer I was working at summer camp when out of the blue, there he was. And he wanted to get back together with me. I stuck to my resolve and told him that I only wanted to be friends. That I'd moved on. He said okay, but then the following weekend he tried to kill himself. There isn't much else in this world that I can imagine inflicting the same intense feeling of guilt upon a person as this. He had left me a note saying that he was going to do this because I had rejected him and his desire to be together again.

It felt like a knife in my heart.

I carried this knife around for such a long time. It had been almost six years by that summer in England. I could not forgive myself for what I felt I had done to my ex-boyfriend. I saw it as my fault. After all, he chose to try and kill himself because I just wanted to be friends.

And I never thought that guilt would leave me.

That week, as I sat listening to this man talk to us about sin and repentance and restitution, the weight of the guilt I felt was becoming a heavier and heavier physical weight pushing down upon my shoulders. For two days I could think of nothing else. But what could I do? I was in anguish. I was convinced this was my cross to bear so what was I supposed to do? I wanted it gone, but how?

Every day, halfway through the morning lecture time we had a half hour break. That Wednesday morning I ran out of the lecture room to take a walk down the long driveway of the mission base. I had to get out of that room. I had to be alone with God. I had to cry. It was all too much for me to handle and the weight of it was only getting worse! I cried my way down that driveway.

Cried tears and cried out from my heart.

God help me!

As I was coming back up the drive, I finally told God that I couldn't do this anymore. I could not carry this guilt around with me another moment. I wanted to be freed from it. Then I asked God to take it from me.

And you know what?

HE DID!

I had been walking almost bent over because of the weight I felt pushing down on me. And then it was just gone! The physical weight was gone and the emotional and spiritual heaviness I had been carrying around were gone too! Immediately I was able to stand up straight and lift my head up! And I specifically remember thinking that if I wanted to I could flap my arms and start flying around! It was amazing! The tears that were still there became ones of joy!

I did stop crying though.

Were my guilt and pain really gone or was that just a momentary experience? I thought through the suicide attempt, and all that I knew I had felt about it for the last six years, and it did nothing to me.

No more guilt.

No more pain.

I still knew complete joy and freedom!

There are a lot of things that happen in our lives that can leave us burdened with guilt, shame, and heaviness. And it is easy to think we have to carry that around, or that there is no other choice than to do so. See, there is an enemy to our souls who wants to keep us burdened with guilt, shame and heaviness. He wants us to walk through life feeling defeated, small, trapped and inhibited.

But he is feeding us a lie!

For we have been given complete freedom from all sin and brokenness because Jesus loves us enough to take those things from us and carry them for us! Because of Jesus, we can live free, abundant and joy filled lives.

"Now the Lord is the Spirit, and where the Spirit of the Lord is, there is freedom" (2 Corinthians 3:17).

"It is for freedom that Christ has set us free. Stand firm, then, and do not let yourselves be burdened again by a yoke of slavery" (Galatians 5:1).

We have been set free. And we need to remember that truth because it is so easy to take back those things that we have been set free from. I had to surrender my guilt and heaviness to God, giving up control of what I was holding onto, in order to experience his amazing freedom. There are things that I need to repeatedly give up to him because I keep taking them back. And sometimes we hold onto things because, at least, that is a known experience, and we are fearful of the unknown.

But the truth remains: Jesus has set us free and we can know that freedom in real, tangible ways. Because God is bigger than we are, more powerful than any of our experiences of pain. And he is right here with us to help us when we ask. He does not want to force himself upon us, but wants us to come to him. When we do, amazing things happen!

I went back into the lecture room a different person. I am sure there was a smile on my face for the rest of the morning. I had been set free! And I had to share my experience. We cannot keep those things to ourselves. They need to be shared to encourage others in their journey, and to mark them or make them official in our own lives. When we share moments like that we allow other people to celebrate with us, to be able to remind us of our newfound selves and freedom.

It was hard to get up there in front of everyone, but the next morning I did just that. I made myself vulnerable and told my story of burden and freedom.

And we all rejoiced.

And we were all encouraged.

And we were all drawn closer to our God who sets us all free.

Chapter Four:
Personal Application

EXERCISE 1

What burden are you carrying around with you that you need to surrender to God? What memory or experience holds you in bondage and keeps you from living a fuller, more purposeful life? Sometimes these things can be the hardest to admit to ourselves, but it is important to start getting them out. Begin by writing about it in a journal or talking with a close friend. Getting things into the light of day is a huge help in dispelling the darkness of the burden. Then spend time alone or with your friend in prayer, asking for God's help in letting it go.

EXERCISE 2

Along with the verses above from 1 Corinthians and Galatians, take time to meditate and pray through the following verses.

Psalm 56:13 — *"For you have delivered me from death and my feet from stumbling, that I may walk before God in the light of life."*

Psalm 116:16 — *"O Lord, truly I am your servant; I am your servant, the son of your maidservant; you have freed me from my chains."*

Psalm 118:5-6 — *"In my anguish I cried to The Lord, and he answered by setting me free. The Lord is with me; I will not be afraid. What can man do to me?"*

Isaiah 61:1-3 — *"The Spirit of the Sovereign Lord is on me, because The Lord has anointed me to preach good news to the poor. He has sent me to bind up the brokenhearted, to proclaim freedom for the captives and release from darkness for the prisoners, to proclaim the year of the Lord's favor and the day of vengeance of our god, to comfort all who mourn, and provide for those who grieve in Zion - to bestow on them a crown of beauty instead of ashes, the oil of gladness instead of mourning, and a garment of praise instead of a spirit of despair. They will be called oaks of righteousness, a planting of The Lord for the display of his splendor."*

John 8:36 — *"So if the Son sets you free, you will be free indeed."*

2 Corinthians 3:17-18 — *"Now The Lord is the Spirit, and where the Spirit of The Lord is, there is freedom. And we, who with unveiled faces all reflect the Lord's glory, are being transformed into his likeness with ever-increasing glory, which comes from The Lord, who is the Spirit."*

Hebrews 4:15-16 — *"For we do not have a high priest who is unable to sympathize with our weaknesses, but we have one who has been tempted in every way, just as we are - yet was without sin. Let us then approach the throne of grace with confidence, so that we may receive mercy and find grace to help us in our time of need."*

James 4:7-8a — *"Submit yourselves, then, to God. Resist the devil, and he will flee from you. Come near to God and he will come near to you."*

EXERCISE 3

Look at a situation that weighs heavily on your soul. What are the lies you believe about yourself and your life because of this? Perhaps you need to share this with another person who can help point out those lies to you. Search the Bible for scripture that reveals the truth you need to know in order to transform your beliefs about yourself. Pray through these verses. Write them out and put them in place you'll see every day as a constant reminder.

CHAPTER FIVE
Standing on the Edge of a Cliff

I am a person who has always had a lot of fears. Fear of the dark. Fear of eternity. Fear of dogs. Fear of strange men. Fear of heights, small spaces, spiral staircases in old castles, falling, flying, swimming in oceans…the list is long and ridiculous.

That summer in England I found myself overwhelmed by a fear of my future. Would I be single my whole life? Would I never have children like I really wanted to? Would God want me to be a missionary my whole life? Would he make me live in Africa? What would I do with my life if I went back home?

I felt consumed with this fear of what I would do with my life.

I had no idea what to do and felt like I was going to go crazy if I didn't get it all worked out. I had no peace. I felt restless and on the edge. And I kept seeing this picture of me in my mind during our lectures, during worship, when I prayed, and I probably dreamed about it. In this picture I am standing on the very edge of an eternal cliff and all I can see in front of me is pitch-black darkness. A pitch-black darkness that I felt I could fall into at any moment. And in this picture, the dark space in front of me was my future.

It paralyzed me.

It caused me to panic and to fight in my spirit.

I really knew no peace of mind during this time as I considered this image and my future.

As with many things though, I kept taking this image and all my fears to God in prayer. During my private prayer time and when praying with others, I kept bringing this before God. Asking him to show me what I was supposed to do and where I was supposed to be. I wanted specifics and I wanted them now!

I am so thankful though that this is not what God gives us. I would most likely have freaked out if God had shown me what was to come in the next few years because I wasn't ready to know those things yet. I was not the person I needed to be in order to do those things. But God did show me something that was exactly what I needed.

One morning in prayer as I once again came to God for help with my future, I saw the same picture of me standing on the very edge of this eternal cliff.

But the darkness was gone.

And in its place was the most brilliant, glorious light! I was standing on the edge of this cliff looking out at a light so beautiful it left me in awe. And I knew this light was God. God was in my future.

God was my future.

Whatever it was that I would be doing after DTS, or two years from then, or in thirty years, I could rest assured that God would be there. And that was all I needed to know. And that gave me the peace I needed to move forward, to not feel paralyzed by my unknowing.

Now that I think about it, this is another one of those anchors that God gave me to help me through difficult times to come. No matter what, I could go into an experience or time or struggle and know that God was with me. To know that I was not alone. Instead, I was surrounded by God's glorious, powerful and blinding presence.

I was safe and secure.

I could step off that cliff and walk as if on firm ground because it is God that I am with and who is guiding me.

Talk about peace and assurance.

Chapter Five:
Personal Application

EXERCISE 1

Consider your fears. Are there one or two that stand out as the most influential in your life, that you spend a lot of time worrying over or that are keeping you from being who God has created you to be?

Consider 2 Corinthians 10:5b which says to *"take captive every thought to make it obedient to Christ."* How do we take thoughts captive to Christ? Create a visual in your mind of you approaching the throne upon which Jesus is seated as King. Take your thought, your fear, and picture yourself placing it down before Jesus. Then, in your mind, picture yourself turning and walking away without that thought or fear. You are free from it and it belongs to Jesus. I imagine, back in the day when kings fought other kings and took prisoners and spoils of war home, that the things brought back, the captives, were paraded before the victorious king for him to see what was now his. And I think that this is what we do with our sins, our fears, and all the things of this world that keep us from living an abundant life in Christ. Jesus is our victorious king over the spoils of his war with Satan. He is king over our sin, our fear, our brokenness. We lay these things down before him and walk away because he fought on our behalf and won. He has taken them captive. We just need to hand them over to him. Ask God to help you give your fears to him and to deepen your trust in him as you do so.

EXERCISE 2

Is there something you have always dreamed of doing with your life that you've never quite had the guts to try? What is it that's holding you back? Sometimes it is legitimately our circumstances that keep us from our dreams (having young children, being in the midst of a current obligation with a job or course of study...), but given time, prayer and allowing God to work out the details, that kind of hinderance can go away. And that just leaves the fears we have that hold us back. Spend time praying through your dreams for your life. Ask God to show you if there is something he wants you to do and if there are issues of fear that need to be worked through before those dreams can be realized. James 1:5 promises that *"If any of you lacks wisdom, he or she should ask God, who gives generously to all without finding fault, and it will be given to him."* God wants us to become who he is creating us to be and he will help us along that path if we ask and are open to his working in our hearts and minds.

EXERCISE 3

Write out and pray through the following verses on fear:

> Psalm 23:4 — *"Even though I walk through the valley of the shadow of death, I will fear no evil, for you are with me; your rod and your staff, they comfort me."*

> Psalm 27:1 — *"The Lord is my light and my salvation - whom shall I fear? The Lord is the stronghold of my life - of whom shall I be afraid?"*

Psalm 34:4 — *"I sought The Lord, and he answered me; he delivered me from all my fears."*
Psalm 139:23-24 — *"Search me, O God, and know my heart; test me and know my anxious thoughts. See if there is any offensive way in me and lead me in the way everlasting."*

Proverbs 29:25 — *"Fear of man will prove to be a snare, but whoever trusts in The Lord is kept safe."*

Isaiah 41:10 — *"So do not fear, for I am with you; do not be dismayed, for I am your God. I will strengthen you and help you; I will uphold you with my righteous right hand."*

2 Thessalonians 3:3 — *"But The Lord is faithful, and he will strengthen and protect you from the evil one."*

1 Peter 5:7 — *"Cast all your anxiety on him because he cares for you."*

1 John 4:18 — *"There is no fear in love. But perfect love drives out fear, because fear has to do with punishment. The one who fears is not made perfect in love."*

CHAPTER SIX
More Waves

There are times though when we need God to remind us of his truths over and over before they settle in and change us. And sometimes they need to hit us over the head before we learn. There was one day during our DTS where we went to another YWAM base to hear the head of YWAM England and the wife of the founder of YWAM speak. I really didn't want to go, and definitely did not want to be there once we arrived. The other base is much bigger and there were a LOT of people around. When I am struggling with an issue I tend to get irritated by everyone around me. This day was no exception.

I was struggling with my future again. Who am I? What am I going to do with my life?

I don't remember what the head of YWAM England talked about that night except that it had to do with us being waves upon the world. Waves of people going out to touch all the nations for the glory of God. I am sure it was a good message, but I was not in the mood.

But I found myself obsessing with the idea of waves the next day during our morning lecture. I was still in that unsettled mood and could not let this idea of waves go. God, in his grace, used that time to speak to me. He tends to do that when I am unsettled. And he used the concept of ocean waves again. He tends to do that too.

Waves.

I remembered the waves at Tintagel and what God revealed to me there.

Waves.

I am supposed to be a wave for God in this world.

I am a wave.

I'm a wave.

This was my thinking that morning condensed into a few lines. Then something struck me. I AM a wave. "Jennifer" means "white wave". The meaning of my name has always been something important to me. I have always known that it holds meaning to my life.

I am a white wave.

Then I looked down at the t-shirt I happened to be wearing that day. And I was amazed at God's timing, his sense of humor and the interesting ways in which he speaks to us. When I lived in Chicago a group of friends and I formed a Celtic interest group. We did various things together like celebrating St. Patrick's Day with authentic Irish food, sharing music and planning a Celtic themed worship service for the seminary there. When I moved home to come to England, they gave me a few things, including the t-shirt that I happened to be wearing that day.

It had a Celtic style wave on it and said, "Celtic Wave".

My jaw probably dropped. I do not believe in coincidences and knew that this was a moment when God was speaking to me. I am a Celtic wave, because "Jennifer" is a Celtic name meaning "white wave".

Once God had my complete attention, I began considering what he might be trying to say to me. My mind was racing all over the place, trying to find a connection between me being a wave and what my future held for me. One of the things I did was to open my Bible and look up the word "wave" in the concordance. I looked up all the verses that contained the word "wave" and found this in Mark:

"Jesus got up, rebuked the wind and said to the waves, 'Quiet! Be still!'"

I sat dumbfounded for a while and then read the whole section the verse comes from. It is the story of Jesus and the disciples going out onto the lake in a boat. Jesus falls asleep while "a furious squall came up" causing the disciples to panic. They wake Jesus up and he commands the wind and waves to be quiet and still. He then asks his disciples, "Why are you so afraid? Do you still have no faith?"

God had my total focus now.

He had shown me that he is my future. That my future holds his glorious presence. And now he was telling me to be quiet and still. To not be afraid and to have faith in him. And I knew that if the wind and the waves could obey him, I could too. Not that this happened over night because sometimes these things are a process. But at that point I was moving forward with a clear message from God that my future and all that I was to be is in his hands. And for that time, I was to be silent and still and allow him to work in me.

I had no idea who Jennifer Hokanson was really supposed to be. I'd believed a lot of lies about who I was, but he was giving me truth. And telling me to be still so he could work in me and show me in his time all that I wanted and needed to know.

He was also setting the stage for future assurance or affirmation. That first summer I had my direction: to be silent and still so that God could work in me. So my faith could grow. So I could not be so afraid. And I think I was able to do that over the next year because the following summer, when I went back to YWAM to help run a DTS at the same base in England, God used this same imagery to speak to me.

During our first week there, those of us leaders were receiving leadership training while we prepared for our students to arrive. At that point I still had no idea what life held for me. But I was continuing to go where I saw God lead and to be open to the work he wanted to do in and through me.

So, that first week, we spent quite a bit of time as a leadership team building each other up and getting ready to lead. One day we were praying after a time of teaching.

We prayed for each of us individually for a time, taking note of images and verses that people received for each person during prayer. One of my co-leaders was a woman I had just met a few days before, Nina. As they were praying for me, she said she saw a picture for me.

It was of an ocean.

I smiled. She said it was of an ocean that was completely at rest.

Clear.

No waves.

It was still.

I had to laugh. And praise God! And thank him for telling me that the raging wave I had been the summer before had finally learned to be quiet! And still! He used that picture, told to me through someone who had no idea about what God had shown me the summer before, to let me know that I was okay. That I had listened and obeyed. That I was on the right track. And I was at peace. Enjoying the beautiful radiance that is my right now and my future. I didn't need to know anything else but that.

Now, Nina also shared that the quiet of the ocean she saw was of one that was a calm before the storm. And a storm was definitely about to hit that summer, but that is another story for a little later in my telling. The important thing here is that I was learning to trust God with my life, my self, my future. I was becoming more settled with who

I am, even if I had no idea who that was. With where I was going, even if I had no idea where that was specifically. God was revealing his goodness and trustworthiness to me and those are two things I would need not only for all of life, but for tough times of healing ahead.

I am a wave.

A white, Celtic wave.

And I was learning to listen to and trust in the voice of God in my life. Without that voice, and without listening to it, all I am is a crashing force blowing this way and that with no purpose or direction. Thank you God for helping me learn to be quiet and still.

Chapter Six:
Personal Application

EXERCISE 1

Where do you see God asking you to turn your focus upon him? Where is he asking you to trust in him and his timing? Where do you need to be quiet and still so that God can work in you, reveal himself to you, or give you direction for your life? Take time to consider these questions and journal your thoughts and/or share them with someone. Pray, asking God to open the eyes of your heart to what he wants to show you. Practice sitting in silence before him, opening yourself up before the Lord as one who desires to hear from him. Write down what you see or hear him revealing to you.

EXERCISE 2

Knowing what the Bible has to say about who God is and how trustworthy he is is important in being able to turn our complete focus upon him with our whole lives so that he can work in us and through us. Meditate on the following verses, allowing the truth contained within them to seep into your soul.

> Deuteronomy 7:9 — "*Know therefore that The Lord your God is God; he is the faithful God, keeping his covenant of love to a thousand generations of those who love him and keep his commands.*"

> 1 Chronicles 29:10b-13 — "*Praise be to you, O Lord, God of our father Israel, from everlasting to*

everlasting. Yours, O Lord, is the greatness and the power and the glory and the majesty and the splendor, for everything in heaven and earth is yours. Yours, O Lord, is the kingdom; you are exalted as head over all. Wealth and honor come from you; you are the ruler of all things. In your hands are strength and power to exalt and give strength to all. Now, our God, we give you thanks, and praise your glorious name."

Psalm 18:1-3, 30-36 — *"I love you, O Lord, my strength. The Lord is my rock, my fortress and my deliverer; my God is my rock, in whom I take refuge. He is my shield and the horn of my salvation, my stronghold. I call to The Lord, who is worthy of praise, and I am saved from my enemies...As for God, his way is perfect; the word of The Lord is flawless. He is a shield for all who take refuge in him. For who is God besides The Lord? And who is the Rock except our God? It is God who arms me with strength and makes my feet like the feet of a deer; he enables me to stand on the heights. He trains my hands for battle; my arms can bend a bow of bronze. You give me your shield of victory, and your right hand sustains me; you stoop down to make me great. You broaden the path beneath me, so that my ankles do not turn."*

Psalm 37:3-7 — *"Trust in The Lord and do good; dwell in the land and enjoy safe pasture. Delight yourself in The Lord and he will give you the desires of your heart. Commit your way to The Lord; trust in him and he will do this: He will make your righteousness shine like the dawn, the justice of your cause like the noonday sun. Be still before The Lord and wait patiently for him; do not fret when men succeed in their way, when they carry out their wicked schemes."*

Psalm 46:1-3 — *"God is our refuge and strength, an ever-present help in trouble. Therefore we will not fear, though the earth give way and the mountains fall into the heart of the sea, though its waters roar and foam and the mountains quake with their surging."*

Psalm 95:1-7 — *"Come, let us sing for joy to The Lord; let us shout aloud to the Rock of our salvation. Let us come before him with thanksgiving and extol him with music and song. For The Lord is the great God, the great King above all gods. In his hand are the depths of the earth, and the mountain peaks belong to him. The sea is his, for he made it, and his hands formed the dry land. Come, let us bow down in worship, let us kneel before The Lord our Maker; for he is our God and we are the people of his pasture, the flock under his care."*

Proverbs 3:5-6 — *"Trust in The Lord with all your heart and lean not on your own understanding; in all your ways acknowledge him, and he will make your paths straight."*

Jeremiah 32:17 — *"Ah, Sovereign Lord, you have made the heavens and the earth by your great power and outstretched arm. Nothing is too hard for you."*

Titus 3:4-7 — *"But when the kindness and love of God our Savior appeared, he saved us, not because of righteous things we had done, but because of his mercy.*

He saved us through the washing of rebirth and renewal by the Holy Spirit, whom he poured out on us generously through Jesus Christ our Savior, so that, having been justified by his grace, we might become heirs having the hope of eternal life."

Hebrews 4:15-16 — *"For we do not have a high priest who is unable to sympathize with our weaknesses, but we have one who has been tempted in every way, just as we are - yet was without sin. Let us then approach the throne of grace with confidence, so that we may receive mercy and find grace to help us in our time of need."*

Revelation 4:8b — *"Holy, holy, holy is The Lord God Almighty, who was, and is, and is to come."*

EXERCISE 3

One great way to grow our trust in the Lord is to worship him. Not only are we putting our whole focus upon him when we worship, but we are also hearing the truths that the worship songs contain about who God is. The more we sing these, and hear these, the more the truth will sink into our being. Put on a worship CD while you clean, cook or work. Take time to do nothing but sing in worship. Get together with other people who are worshipping in song and allow the truth of who God is to settle deep within your heart and mind.

CHAPTER SEVEN
Grace Tickets

When my DTS went to the other YWAM base I did listen to what the wife of the founder of YWAM had to say. What she shared was a message that has helped me not only with the ordinary things of life, but the bigger, tougher times of pain and healing as well.

She talked to us about the idea of "Grace Tickets". The idea is this: each day each of us is given the grace we need for that day and that day alone. We do not receive grace for tomorrow, or a year from today, or ten years from today. Just today. We can only live in one time and that is today, right now. Therefore we only get what we need for the right now. The today.

Why is this important and helpful?

Because if we live with this idea in mind it takes away the need to worry. I cannot worry about tomorrow, how things will go, if I will be able to do that difficult task that looms ahead, because I am not there yet. I am in today and today does not contain what tomorrow will. I could not worry about the unknown of our fast approaching outreach in London because we were still living in the countryside doing the lecture phase of the DTS. I could not worry about what job I would have when I moved home because I was still in England doing missionary work. I could not worry about whether or not my future husband would understand my quirks or want to handle money the same way as me because at that point I was single. I could not worry about the idea of getting back on a plane to go home, since I have a fear of flying, because that was several months away.

I am not sharing this idea of a Grace Ticket to say that we are not to consider our future, or how we will handle various people, situations and difficulties. I am saying though that we can have incredible peace, given to us by God, by focusing on today.

By leaning on God for today.

By looking to him for what we need in the moment we need it, not ten days before we need it.

Not even the night before.

God is a great provider God who cares deeply about us and all of our needs. He knows what we need even before we do. And if we can trust him to provide for us daily, to give his grace daily, then we can live with a lot more peace and a lot less needless worry.

One of my biggest worries on my DTS was knowing that we would likely have to do street evangelism once we got to London. Sure enough, we got our schedule for our first few weeks there and found out that we would be spending a whole day doing evangelism in Leicester Square right in the center of busy, touristy London. My gut instinct sent me into a complete panic! I am not an outgoing person. Evangelism is not a gift of mine. Talking with complete strangers is not something I am good at. I also do not like being forced to do something that I do not want to do!

This was real fear.

But I had Grace Tickets on my mind.

None of the days leading up to our Leicester Square Street Evangelism were days that included the grace, the provision, the help to do street evangelism. Those days included grace for other things like team building exercises, cleaning toilets, listening to lectures. So I tried to remember this idea and not worry.

And I found that it worked.

The idea of what I would have to do in London would pop into my head, I would acknowledge it and set it aside. That was not for today.

The day did arrive though. I think I would normally have been freaking out all morning as we got ready, had breakfast, had a morning meeting, and whatever else we did before leaving, but I was okay. It was The Day for Leicester Square, and I was going to be fine. Because I also found that I could say while in that specific day, that when I was not actually in Leicester Square doing the street evangelism I did not have the grace yet to do it. But I knew I would be fine once we got there. God would show me what to do and help me to do it.

It was actually quite an amazing day. After I got dressed that morning I went out into the garden attached to the church we were staying in to read my Bible and prepare myself for the day. I happened to be reading in the book of Psalms and read a psalm that was used in a song my church in Chicago would sing:

"Give thanks to the Lord, call on his name; make known among the nations what he has done. Sing to him, sing praise to him; tell of all his wonderful acts. Glory in his holy name; let the hearts of those who seek the Lord rejoice." (Psalm 105:1-3).

As soon as I read those verses the song filled my heart and my mind and I could not get it out. I found myself quietly singing or humming the song from that moment on and throughout the outreach that day. It has a circular quality, wrapping around on itself so that once I reached the end I found myself back at the beginning. It could go on eternally, and it did for me that day. The song was a kind of grace, or peace, to me as it gave me something to focus on. And as it allowed me to be continually worshipping God throughout all I did that day.

My focus was on God. My heart was turned toward him and even though I was nervous about what I would have to do once we got to Leicester Square, I was in a place where I knew I would do whatever God asked of me.

We finally set out, going to a building near Leicester Square where we met up with a larger team we had been working with for the past few weeks. The man leading us that day took us through a training time to show us what would happen and to prepare us for our part in it. This man was an artist, a story teller and a powerful evangelist. He had a way of sharing basic principles and ideas about us, God, our sin, Jesus and our need for salvation.

He would start with a large empty board on a stand. He would paint a few random shapes or words on that board while waiting for a crowd to gather around him. Then he would begin his story. He would tell the story of our sin and separation from God. Of our need for reconciliation with God. Of Jesus' role in bringing us back into a right relationship with God. And of the life that we can now lead because of that. As he talked, he would continue painting on the board, filling in the shapes and words so that in the end he had a completed picture that told the whole story. It really was quite amazing to see him do this.

Well, once he finished with his part, he would invite people to stay and talk with him if they wanted to. And, when he finished, our job was to turn to the person next to us and ask them what they thought about what they had heard. To engage them in conversation about the ideas the man had talked about. And it worked. And it worked well. We were working that day with a group of people from a local church so that if anyone became interested in checking out a church, or finding out more about Jesus, or acknowledged their need for Jesus in order to have a right relationship with God, they could be given a place to go and do that.

Once I knew that I was expected to turn to complete strangers and ask them about what they thought about the man's message, my heart skipped several beats!

I freaked out! Could I really do that? I wanted to because that was what I was there to do. But I was scared.

The song I had been singing was still there though, drawing me back to God and I had a certain amount of peace in the midst of my panic. I knew that I would have the grace, the ability, to do this. All I had to do was keep my focus on God and let him give that grace to me.

Let him work in me.

Let him provide.

I could do this.

We finally set out for Leicester Square and the man set up his board, painting his initial shapes and words. A crowd began to gather, because this is an area of London where a lot of street performers go. This is an area where people expect to see a lot of different activities going on around them for their entertainment or interest. When he felt there were enough people there, he started in with his story. And while he talked, I prayed.

God, show me what to do.

God, lead me to the right person to talk with.

The more I prayed, the more I knew I was supposed to be praying. And when the man finished his talking and people around me started talking with each other about what he'd said, I kept on praying. I knew that was what I was brought there to do that day. I prayed for the conversations I saw happening all around me. I prayed for my friends, that they would be able to listen well and to share about Jesus with those they were talking with in a way that was clear and real. I prayed for those they were talking to. For the man I watched accept Jesus into his life right there in front of me. I prayed that people would desire to know God. Desire to be reconciled to him in a real, passionate, life-giving relationship. I prayed that there would be no distractions from these good conversations.

I prayed. God brought me there that day to pray.

And I had peace about that. Incredible peace. All that worrying I could have done would have been a waste of my time! Because God brought me there to pray. My friends told me at the end of the day that they were so encouraged in their conversations because they could see me and knew that I was praying for them. They knew me. Knew that prayer is a passion of mine. And knew that I was lifting them up before God. They received grace from that and were able to share about the great conversations they had because of it.

And that was just round one!

After a while, I could see conversations were dying down. People were moving away and on to the things they were doing that day. And I saw that our speaker was setting up for another time of painting, of storytelling and of conversation.

My song was still going on and on in my mind. In my heart. Rejoice, in the Lord, Rejoice in the Lord! Let the hearts of those who seek the Lord rejoice…Rejoice in the Lord, Rejoice in the Lord…as I was singing God told me to do something to help prepare for the next round. Now, when I say "God told me to", in this instance I mean that at some point I just knew that he wanted me to do something special. He had put an idea in my mind and I knew with all my heart that he was guiding me to do this thing.

In the story of the people of Israel taking the city of Jericho, God tells them to walk around the city for seven days, one time each day. On the seventh day of doing this God delivered the city into their hands. Their walking around the city was a way of claiming the city for God. Of staking that territory for him. Of being his presence in that place. I had recently read that story in my Bible reading and in that moment I knew I was supposed to do something similar in Leicester Square. I needed to walk around our area seven times praying and singing my song to God to mark it as his place. To invite him to be present. To ask for his peace to reign there while the speaker spoke and we had conversations.

So I did. In the middle of Leicester Square I walked in a circle seven times singing my never-ending song about the hearts of those seeking God rejoicing. I was rejoicing in God!

And an incredible thing happened! It was as if God had come down and through my walking and praying and singing had built an invisible wall around the area we were in. I say this because one of two things happened. Either people would walk toward this "wall", hit it and go out of their way to walk around it and keep going, or people would enter into it and completely stop in their tracks and enter this area of peace and the presence of God. The peace was almost tangible. I noticed it and so did a number of my friends. God carved out this little area for himself in order to create the perfect place for people to stop, listen and have conversation about him and themselves. It was an amazing thing to be a part of.

I have to tell a little, funny aside here. While I knew that God had brought me there that day to pray, I still felt a little guilty for not having at least tried to talk with anyone like we were supposed to. So, at the end of the second round I decided to try and talk with the guy standing next to me. I turned and asked, "So, what did you think about what the man was sharing?" But the guy wasn't interested in talking about that. All he wanted was my phone number so we could go out sometime! I quickly ended the conversation and laughed.

I was worried about having to talk to strangers. God brought me there to pray. But I had stepped out and tried to talk anyway and all that happened is a strange guy hit on me. I need to stick to what I know God is telling me to do, what he is giving me the grace to do, and nothing else.

My Grace Ticket that day included courage to be open to doing whatever God asked me to do. A song to sing and prayers to pray. The peace to listen to his voice telling me to walk around that area seven times. The ability to laugh at myself when I decided to do my own thing and got hit on. And the incredible joy that came from worshipping God through all that we did!

That experience helped me to lean on the idea of the Grace Ticket on other days and with other issues. When the day came to say good-bye to all my new, incredible friends, I was able to. When I had to get on an airplane five days after the tragic events of 9/11 to fly back home. When I realized that it was time for me to start telling people that I had been sexually abused. When I recognized that my belief that I would stay single because there was something wrong with me on the inside was a lie that I had to face. When I realized that I did not know if I could ever truly trust a man completely. When I was faced with the unknown of what to do with my life.

In all of these things, I was learning to lean on God for what I needed, knowing that he would give me all I needed in order to go through them. In the face of deep pain and fear I was able to have peace and the secure knowledge that I could make it through because I had God and he was taking care of me.

Giving me the grace to deal with each day as it came.

No more. No less.

The Bible tells us that God's grace is sufficient for us and that there is a peace from God that passes all understanding when we lift our needs up to him. It also says that we need not be anxious about anything and to trust in him with all of our hearts. This is what it means to believe God will give us grace for each day in that day, and to live like we know it will happen.

Chapter Seven:
Personal Application

EXERCISE 1

Look back on your list of fears and issues that worry you. How many of them are not about things you are dealing with right now, today? Are they concerns about possible future events that you can apply the idea of a Grace Ticket to? As you consider Grace Tickets, does that help ease the fear or worry you have about them? Spend time in prayer, alone or with a trusted friend, asking God to help you embrace this idea. Asking him to help you live fully in the day you are in, knowing that God will help you face the things of the future when they happen, in the future.

EXERCISE 2

Create a Grace Ticket as a tangible reminder of this concept. Create something on your computer and print it out. Draw a ticket with pencils or crayons. Have one that you keep in a prominent place to remind you of what it stands for. Keep a stack in an easily accessible place and write on the back of each one the fear or worry that is on your mind and symbolically set it aside until the day that you face that fear or worry. Sometimes physical actions help to impress spiritual truths into our thinking.

EXERCISE 3

Memorize the following verses as reminders of God's sufficiency and provision of peace when we surrender our anxieties to him.

Matthew 6:33-34 — *"But seek first his kingdom and his righteousness, and all these things will be given to you as well. Therefore do not worry about tomorrow, for tomorrow will worry about itself. Each day has enough trouble of its own."*

2 Corinthians 12:9 — *"But he said to me, 'My grace is sufficient for you, for my power is made perfect in weakness.' Therefore I will boast all the more gladly about my weaknesses, so that Christ's power may rest on me."*

Philippians 4:6-7 — *"Do not be anxious about anything but in everything, by prayer and petition, with thanksgiving, present your requests to God. And the peace of God, which transcends all understanding, will guard your hearts and your minds in Christ Jesus."*

EXERCISE 4

The story of Daniel and his time in the lions' den is a good one to look at in terms of "Grace Tickets." It is an extreme example, but perhaps looking at someone who's trust in God got him through such extreme circumstances will help us to have greater faith no matter how big or small our own situation is.

Daniel was one of the Israelites taken captive to Babylon. Because of his good character and God's favor, he became someone of high leadership in both the Babylonian and Medo-Persian Empires. At the point in his life that we're going to consider he had been chosen as one of three *"administrators to supervise the princes and to watch out for the king's interests."* (Daniel 6:2 NLT). The Bible then tells us that he so distinguished himself above all the other princes and administrators that they plotted to find a way to discredit him. Upon realizing they could find no fault in how he lived his life and conducted business, they said, *"Our only chance of finding grounds for accusing Daniel will be in connection with the requirements of his religion."* (6:5). They proposed a law to King Darius which stated that for one month the only one who could be prayed to was King Darius and the lions' den would be where lawbreakers would end up. Daniel, however, continued to pray to God three times a day as he was used to doing, which was exactly what the evil plotters had hoped. They turned Daniel in as a breaker of the new law and King Darius had no choice but to put him in the lions' den. Expecting the worst, the king went to the lions' den and called for Daniel. And he answered! In verse 21 Daniel says, *"My God sent his angel to shut the lions' mouths so that they would not hurt me, for I have been found innocent in his sight."* How amazing is that! In the end, the people who plotted against Daniel were thrown with their families into the lions's den and immediately torn apart, and King Darius recognized the God of the Israelites as the living God and the one to fe feared (6:26).

Where in this story do we see Daniel living with his daily Grace Tickets? There are several aspects of this story that point to his complete reliance upon God for all that he needs in the moment he needs it. First of all, he could have despaired of life once taken captive to Babylon, but he didn't. Instead he continued to remain faithful to God in the foreign land, surrounded by foreign customs and religious practices. He did not try to conform to the way of living around him as he entered the political life there, but maintained his integrity before God and worship of him.

Secondly, and very much related to the first example, he maintained his practice of daily prayer. Three times a day, the Bible says, he went to his room to pray. He was keeping the lines of communication open with God. Continuing in worship of him. Allowing God to fill him and speak to him so that he would be prepared and ready for whatever came his way.

Thirdly, despite knowing that he would be caught, turned in and made lion food, he continued to be faithful to God and to pray to him. His trust in God, and reliance upon him for all things, was more important to him than anything else. And he knew that no matter what happened God would be with him and help him. That's not to say that it was guaranteed that God would keep him alive, but that was not what mattered most. He went to the lions' den in full confidence that God was with him no matter what.

And finally, God did rescue him. He did send an angel to shut the mouths of the lions and spared Daniel's life. And he came out without a scratch and praising God.

Do you have faith like Daniel? Do you rely upon God to help you in each situation? Or do you waste time worrying and trying to fix things yourself. Spend some time meditating on this Bible story. What strikes you the most? Where are you feeling challenged by Daniel's example? What changes can you make right now to start living as he did, having full confidence in God's daily provision of grace?

CHAPTER EIGHT
Living in the Opposite Spirit

One final idea I learned that first summer in England has to do with how we face, or enter into, a difficult situation, time, relationship or place. Sometimes we have people in our lives that really stretch our patience. Or there are places that just bring us down. Sap our emotional energy. Frustrate us. There are physical areas we can be in that affect our mood. Or there are things we believe about ourselves that we know are lies but we let them control us.

What do we do when faced with these things?

Sometimes we allow the other person's behavior or mood to change ours so that we become gloomy or end up sharing their anger. We allow the mood of the person or place to take control of us. We let the lies we believe determine decisions we make about our lives and ourselves. Instead of being excited about ministry we get frustrated or apathetic about it. Instead of being filled with the joy of our salvation and new life we get depressed and down about life. And while we should want the love of Jesus for people to guide our interactions and care for them, we get sucked into gossip, anger, bitterness, jealousy and laziness toward others and let that get in the way of relationships and ministry.

Life is not easy. Relationships are tough. We live in a sinful, broken world where bad moods happen.

A world where the person who sets their alarm to go off really early never hears it but the other seven people in the room do. Where people live in fear for their lives. Where homeless people poop on the doorstep of the church you are living in for the summer. Where men grab at women because they see them as objects. Where planes are flown into towers. Where flippant remarks are made in jest but received as slaps in the face. Where other people's issues, or our own, affect our attitudes, our decisions, our lives.

But we don't have to live in such a way that these things control our lives, our moods, our responses to them. We don't have to become defeated by these moods or attitudes or issues with places and people. Because we have the Holy Spirit living within us, guiding us, working in us, giving us the power to live the full life of Jesus.

With the Spirit's help we can learn to come to a situation or relationship in the opposite spirit.

When a person is coming at us with anger, we do not have to give in to that and react in kind. We can still respond and approach that person with love, patience and kindness. The person may still walk away angry, but our loving action toward them may just do something to their heart, their mood, their thinking. And maybe it will just keep us in the right place and away from anger.

Or when there is a place that is difficult to be in. Perhaps it brings back painful memories, or the activities of that place are a temptation for us to join in. If we know this, if we are aware of ourselves and our surroundings, we can come prepared to face what is there. Or we can notice how the place is affecting us and make the decision to leave or take action to stop letting it do so.

The last two thirds of our outreach in London took place in the East End of London. This is a culturally diverse, poorer, immigrant area of London where people in ministry tend to quickly burn out. It is a very hard place to do ministry. There is almost a physically visible line between the eastern edge of the City of London and the East End. When walking over that line things go from the affluent, upbeat and beautiful to the poor, dirty, rundown and oppressive. And we felt that while we were there. It was so easy to go out in the morning, ready for great things, only to very quickly become frustrated with people, apathetic toward everything and depressed because of the gloomy atmosphere there. We would see wonderful things happen in ministry, but walk away down and frustrated with ourselves, the area, the ministry. And whenever we had time to ourselves, it was amazing how quickly we all escaped back to the brighter City of London. We were allowing ourselves to be touched and controlled by the oppressive spirit of that area of London.

So what could we do? What did we do?

There is nothing that quite changes a bad mood to a good one like singing. And praising God in particular. Of course, when you are in that negative place one of the last things you want to do is to sing praise to God, but that is exactly what we needed to do. It would usually start with just a couple of us in the living room area, or in this stairwell that had awesome acoustics. We would start singing quietly and then a few more would join us. Before we knew it a number of us would be in that place together singing at the top of our lungs! We would become immersed in the words, in the presence of God in that place. The truths of what we were singing about life, about who God is, about who we are in him would bring us back to that place of joy, of love, of purpose, of desire to see great things happen for God.

In our singing we would come at the East End of London in the opposite spirit. We would come at the oppression with joy and purpose. We would bring love and passion for Jesus to the apathy and anger of people. We brought acceptance to the outcast. We walked in truth in the face of lies.

Why is this important to my story?

Not only is it a valuable lesson for anyone wanting to live a full and purposeful life, but it was also a necessary one for me to learn as I began facing my past and the lies about myself that I was starting to recognize as such. There were many days that summer, the year following and the years since then that I have become overwhelmed by life. By what was going on around me. And it is always easy to give in and give up. Learning how to come at a situation in the opposite spirit helped me to not give in and give up. It became another tool to use, when faced with pain and difficulty, to deal with myself and my past. And to move forward. To have hope while moving through hurtful memories. To start living out the truth of who I am in Jesus even if I did not believe that truth yet.

It is living proactively.

Purposefully.

It is embracing the victory of Jesus over sin and brokenness and allowing that victory to be made manifest in our lives.

Coming at something in the opposite spirit usually happens for me through meditation of scripture and singing worship to God. As I read my Bible a verse sticks out and becomes my focus for that day. I pray through the verse. I sing it. I draw it out. I get a worship song stuck in my head. In a sense I eat, breathe and sleep that truth of God and allow it to permeate all the areas of my life. In this way my focus, my heart, are turned toward God so that I see and experience life through that lens. I am not perfect at this. But I am aware of the need to live this way. It is always close to the surface of my thinking and there to access when I recognize my need to be living in the opposite spirit.

It became another anchor in my life that summer.

Chapter Eight:
Personal Application

EXERCISE 1

Think about some current areas in your life where you need to live in the opposite spirit. Pick one that you face frequently and find a verse or worship song to focus on when that situation pops up again. Write it out and display it in a prominent place in your home or work. Our draw or paint it out. Having a verse or song imprinted on your mind and heart in advance will help you in the moment you need to use it.

EXERCISE 2

Make a list of other situations in your life where you know you need to start responding differently. Perhaps there is a tough family or work relationship that always leaves you in a funk. Maybe you have an addiction to a food or to shopping that make it difficult to be in certain places or situations. Or the recurring issue with the loud or messy neighbor that is difficult to get along with. Look at this list and take time to come up with creative ways to come at these situations and relationships in the opposite spirit. Organize a neighborhood party to get to know your neighbors better. Find things to celebrate about people that are hard to get along with. Leave encouraging notes for the grumpy person in the office. There are so many things we can do to bring change to people, situations and moods. Ask God to inspire you with creativity and the courage to follow through.

EXERCISE 3

Read Acts 16:16-40 and consider how Paul and Silas responded to their situation by coming at it in the opposite spirit. What stands out to you? If you we're arrested, "*severely flogged*" (v. 23), and then thrown in jail, what do you think your response would be?

How did they respond? Paul and Silas "*were praying and singing hymns to God, and the other prisoners were listening to them*" (v. 25). They must have made a good impression on the other prisoners because when they had the chance to escape after the earthquake, they didn't. Their response to their horrible circumstances was one of joy, and that joy spoke to the other people there and led to the conversion of the jailer and his family. Paul and Silas acting in the opposite spirit to their situation not only effected them, but also the lives of many around them. Again, this is an extreme example of how to live this concept out, but we all face things on a daily basis that we either can allow to control us, or that we can instead be a force for good and change to.

How does this story encourage you? Can you view difficulties and struggle through a new lens?

CHAPTER NINE
A Summer of Preparation

Learning to live like I knew God could provide, guide, give grace, be trustworthy...this is what my first summer in England was about.

I came there initially as a fearful, closed person who wanted to either have control over my future or at least know everything in advance. Through these experiences I've shared God was showing me both that I was not still and telling me to be still. That I was afraid and that I did not have to be afraid. That I could consider my future and the things to come, but not worry about them and how things would play out. That I did not have to give into the difficulty of life, but to live with joy no matter what was going on in or around me. I was learning to let go, open my hands, my arms, my heart and my mind so that God could then reveal and lead and provide for me.

It was a tough summer.

The ideas and experiences I struggled with were hard and self-revealing for me. I was not always happy with life and with myself. I was learning to not be afraid of the future and what God might ask me to do. To trust him with my life and who he was leading me to be. To not try so hard to control life and what happens to me.

But at the same time, it was one of the best summers of my life.

I had taken the challenge of adventure and the unknown that I feared so much and come through it a stronger and more open person. I was learning to be still, to trust and to allow things to happen in God's time. I was learning to take risks and to see and hear from God in new ways. I was learning to see and experience the world through his lens.

I had no idea what I would do when I got home, but I knew life would never be the same.

I was not the same.

And I was finally in the place where God could bring me through the biggest challenge of my life. The most painful and dark place of my life. I did not realize it at the time, but that first summer in England prepared me to begin dealing with the abuse I'd experienced as a child.

Chapter Nine:
Personal Application

EXERCISE 1

If you have been going through this book and doing some or all of the personal application questions, how is your life different now compared to before you started? If you have been journaling, read back through all you've written. How have your struggles changed? How are they the same? Where do you still want to see growth or healing in your life? What victories have you seen in your life? Have you tried new things, responded to people and circumstances differently, has your trust in God grown? Do you know more joy in the midst of life? If you've been going through this with someone, either formally or just a friend you talk with a lot, ask them what changes they see in you. Sometimes it is harder to see how we change and need someone who is more of an observer to our lives. Spend time thanking God for the positive things you take note of and ask him for help with the areas you still struggle with or want to see change in.

CHAPTER TEN
From Darkness to Light

Leaving England and the amazing friends I had made on my DTS to go back home was a very difficult time. It didn't help that our leaving coincided with the week of 9/11. My DTS changed me and 9/11 changed the world. I had no idea what to expect of life back at home. No idea of what I would do. And I spent probably a good month or two in a kind of shock. While it had been difficult learning to share a room with six other women in a large house full of people, I think it was harder to learn how to be at home again. How to sleep in a room by myself. How to keep a life of worship and love for people while apart from others who had gone through the same life-changing experiences. I did not want to just go back to who I had been. Or to the same way of living.

But what could I do? How was I to live now that I was back in wealthy, small-town America?

I had no answers to any of these questions, but I was determined to keep my focus on God to see what he was leading me to do. I worked hard to keep up my times of prayer, worship and Bible study. I continued to practice living with my daily grace tickets and coming at things in the opposite spirit. And I started reading many of the books that had been recommended to us on the DTS. I didn't know what life held for me, but I could keep leaning on God who did know.

And he was leading me, but not to everything that I expected or wanted. About a month after returning home I went to Colorado with my mom for two weeks to visit relatives and family friends. And it was here that God started working in me to face the fact that I had been abused.

I have always remembered what happened to me. At some point in college I put words to it so that I knew I had been sexually abused. But it was never something I thought a lot about. And I certainly never talked about it. I naively thought it was just something bad that had happened to me that had nothing to do with my life since then. I had no idea how much it had affected me, my thoughts, my beliefs, my actions, my person, my relationships.

While in Colorado, my mom and I went to a few places that put the truth of what this person did to me right in front of my face. I did not want to go, but I could not say why since no one else knew and I was not going to say. In not sharing about what had happened to me I thought I was protecting my parents from a hurtful truth about someone they loved. I knew it would devastate them and so saw no need to tell them about it. Why cause them so much hurt if I didn't need to?

But being in those places in Colorado caused me to start fighting and struggling against my abuse. It was put in the forefront of my thinking and I could not stop it from being there. Why, after all these years, was I struggling with this? All of a sudden I could not look at pictures of my abuser. I found myself filled with anger toward him. And full of shame because of what he'd done to me. It makes no sense, but abuse like that can cause the abused person to feel responsible for it. Like it is a reflection upon them or says something about who they are as a person. And these thoughts confused and consumed me. I did not know what to do with them. Or who to turn to besides God.

And I really just wanted it all to magically go away.

There was one night though, soon after I returned home from Colorado, where God kept me up all night. I could not fall asleep. All I could think of was my abuse. My abuser.

Why did this happen?

What was I supposed to do with it?

I did not want to share it with anyone. But God was speaking to me through my thought process that night. As I struggled with all this through the night he began revealing a truth to me that I could not ignore. That night he began showing me the truth of the abuse and how it affected others besides me. At the end of that long and painful night, I knew that it was time to start talking about my abuse. I knew that even though other people did not know about it, it had affected me and them in a way that needed to be faced and dealt with. There was a big secret in the middle of our family that needed to be brought into the light of day.

Not just for the sake of revealing the secret, but in order to dispel the power of that secret over our lives.

Over my life.

And a conversation my mom had with me offered me peace and the desire to move forward in the midst of this confusing time. Not knowing of the struggle within me toward my abuser, she told me about conversations she had had with him years ago, after he had abused me. At some point my abuser had accepted Jesus as his savior. Had accepted the forgiveness that was extended to him. Had accepted the new life that Jesus gives to those who acknowledge their need for him in their life. Who acknowledge Jesus' victory over our sin and its hold on us.

My abuser stood as a forgiven, new person before God.

Forgiven for sins just as I am forgiven.

Loved and cherished as God loves and cherishes me.

When God looks upon my abuser he sees the beauty and perfection of Jesus because Jesus took away his ugliness and sin. Just like when God looks at me.

Knowing this, I knew that in time I could forgive my abuser. I could work through my anger and pain. Knowing this helped motivate me to move forward. To start talking with people about it. It was a grace God gave me. If God, in all his glory and holiness could love my abuser and forgive him his sins, then I knew that with his help I could reach that same place of love and forgiveness.

Knowing I needed to start talking did not make it a reality for a while though. Knowing you have to do something really difficult does not make the doing of that thing easy. But I was finally able to start sharing about my abuse with a few close friends. People who were separate from my abuser and could offer me love, tears, a listening ear and walk with me in my anger, shame and pain. They offered me grace and acceptance. They affirmed that I was not to blame. That I was not responsible. That I was a beautiful woman who deserved more than what I had gone through and was living with.

I eventually got up the guts to share what happened with my sister a few weeks after Christmas. She had no idea this had happened. She too offered love and grace to me. And together we started praying and talking about sharing this with our parents. I knew that telling them would be the most difficult, but was comforted by my sister's standing beside me in doing so.

As I told people, as I began sharing my deep, dark secret, I found that it got easier. The hold my abuse had upon me was being removed in the telling. Light was entering the darkness of my life and darkness cannot exist where there is light. I felt a relief to finally be getting this experience out and off my chest.

In March my sister and I were able to sit down with our parents and tell them about my abuse. As anticipated, it was a very hard thing to have to do. Telling your parents that their little girl went through such a horrible thing is gut wrenching. I knew I was breaking their hearts even though I knew I had to tell them. They cried. They held me and loved me. And they really struggled with it in the weeks that followed. But it was a necessary step in the process of healing.

I felt a new freedom and lightness in my life that did not exist before.

It doesn't make sense that we have to experience pain at times in order to find freedom, but that is what had to happen in my life. I had reached a point in my life where I could think about myself and the truth of my abuse without all the secrets and shame and darkness.

I wasn't done dealing with it, but I had taken a very big step toward healing. Now I was facing my abuse in the light of God.

And in the midst of loving community.

Chapter Ten:
Personal Application

EXERCISE 1

All, or most, of us have those events or times in our lives that we keep locked away in our memory because they are too difficult to speak about, or we are just too ashamed to let other people know. Maybe you have been hurt by someone in the past, or are currently being hurt. Maybe you are the one who has done the hurting to another person. Maybe there is an addiction that's taken hold of your life. Whatever it is, no matter how big or small, if you are keeping it locked within the recesses of your mind, or just keeping what you know and have experienced to yourself, it is affecting you. How you view yourself and other people. How you respond to certain situations. It may be holding you captive. We cannot fully walk in God's abundant life if we are keeping things in the dark. Spend some time in thought and prayer. Take a step of courage if you need to and allow yourself to be completely honest with yourself. Is there anything from your past or current situation that you are holding onto that you need to allow in the open? If only just between you and God? Sometimes the first step is the hardest...being honest with yourself and God. But God already knows everything about you and loves you deeply. And he desires to make you whole. To heal your hurts.

If you do have something that comes to mind and are ready to, write about it in your journal. You may have written about a memory or burden that you carry from the section titled "A Burden Lifted." If you have, look back at what you wrote and reflect upon whether or not it still has a hold on you. How have you changed or grown since then? What is still a struggle for you? Sometimes getting things out, even if just in our private journals, is what it takes to get a process of healing started. And if you're ready, talk with a trusted friend. Ask them to pray with you about what happened and about your desire to be freed from this.

EXERCISE 2
Read through and consider what the following verses have to say about God helping you in bringing things from darkness into the light.

2 Samuel 22:29-30 — *"You are my lamp, O Lord; the Lord turns my darkness into light. With your help I can advance against a troop; with my God I can scale a wall."*

Psalm 139:9-12 — *"If I rise on the wings of the dawn, if I settle on the far side of the sea, even there your hand will guide me, your right hand will hold me fast. If I say, 'Surely the darkness will hide me and the light become night around me,' even the darkness will not be dark to you; the night will shine like the day, for darkness is as light to you."*

Isaiah 42:16 — *"I will lead the blind by ways they have not known, along unfamiliar paths I will guide them; I will turn the darkness into light before them and make the rough places smooth. These are the things I will do; I will not forsake them."*

Isaiah 61:1-2 — *"The Spirit of the Sovereign Lord is on me, because The Lord has anointed me to preach good news to the poor. He has sent me to bind up the brokenhearted, to proclaim freedom for the captives and release from darkness for the prisoners, to proclaim the year of the Lord's favor and the day of vengeance of our God, to comfort all who mourn."*

Matthew 4:16 — *"The people living in darkness have seen a great light; on those living in the land of the shadow of death a light has dawned."*

EXERCISE 3

Express yourself by drawing or painting out your thoughts and feelings. This can be a helpful vehicle in sharing your experience and brokenness with another person.

CHAPTER ELEVEN
Removing Knots in the Wood

As I was going through this struggle of sharing my abuse, I was also trying to figure out what to do next with my life. One option was to go back to England in the spring to help run a DTS and it became increasingly obvious that this was what I was supposed to do. My passion continued for the people of England and for the possibility of missionary work there. I applied to participate in the leadership school that helped run the DTS and was accepted. I raised the money I needed and set off for England again that April.

It was great to be back in England and I immediately knew a peace about being there again. Our first week back at the mission base was busy and full of planning, preparation and leadership training. It was during this week that God revealed to me through my friend Nina that I had become the still and calm ocean that he needed me to be. I knew great peace about being there to help lead, excitement for what that summer held for all of us, and a joy to be serving God.

I think I also naively thought that the hardest part of dealing with my abuse was behind me. I didn't realize that there was still a lot to face and deal with.

In one of the first prayer times we had with our students one of them saw an image of a wooden fence when I was being prayed for. She said that the knots in the wood were starting to come out and that God was going to fill the empty spaces with himself so that I would be made whole again. I remember being very confused by what she shared.

What was that supposed to mean?

I didn't feel like I had holes in my life.

But looking back on that summer I know that is exactly what God did for me while in England. There were a lot of lies I believed about myself that needed to be removed from my life so that I could start believing and living the truth of who I am as a child of God made new and perfect.

And it didn't take long for those lies to start becoming apparent to me.

I remember one sunny morning sitting against the fence of the football pitch. I was depressed and unhappy with my life and myself. I was feeling left out because I did not have a boyfriend. I was not married and didn't have kids like so many people I knew. I was having a pity party with myself and becoming more and more angry with what I saw when I compared my life to the lives of women around me. Why was I still single, at the age of 27? Why was I being left behind when all I had ever wanted was to get married and have children?

Was I being punished for something?

What was wrong with me?

This is that moment when I realized I believed that something must be wrong with me on the inside because I knew I was attractive on the outside. There must be some fundamental thing wrong with who I am to make no one want to be with me. And knowing this I felt doomed to always be single because I was only getting older and so soon the one thing I did have going for me would fade and cease to exist.

This was my thinking. It seems silly now. But it caused me great pain and brought many tears.

God was so good to me in the midst of my pain though. He had placed two great women around me that summer to listen to me. To pray with me. To point out the lies I was believing and to instead tell me the truth of who I am. They proclaimed this truth over me. Proclaimed that I am a beautiful woman of God on the inside and the outside. That I have been made new in Jesus Christ. That my sins have been washed away so that God sees the beauty and perfection of Jesus when he looks at me. That I have much to offer to the world around me. That God has great plans for me that may or may not include marriage. That my abuse does not need to continue to define who I am or how I live. That I have been set free from all these lies and experiences to live a victorious life in Jesus through the Holy Spirit.

As they said these truths to me directly, or over me in prayer, they began to take hold of me. To overpower the lies they were replacing and take root in me.

Because I had learned to be still before God, because I was trying to live in the opposite spirit, because I was learning not to fear the future but live with each day's Grace Ticket, I was able to stop believing these lies and instead start living the truths.

The empty holes in my life were being filled in by God's truth.

Chapter Eleven:
Personal Application

EXERCISE 1

If you identified one or more things in the last section about an experience or aspect of your life that is holding you captive, or if you know of specific issues that you struggle with, there are most likely lies that you are believing about yourself. These lies are keeping you from healing, from walking in the freedom that is ours in Christ, and from living the abundant life we are promised. Working on your own or with a friend, spend time thinking and praying about what those lies could be. Ask God to open your eyes to the lies you live. If you know of a verse that speaks the truth you need to hear, write it out. Paint it. Put it in places you will see all the time. Have friends pray the truth over you. Ask God to help you replace the lie with the truth of what his word says.

Hebrews 4:12 says, *"For the word of God is living and active. Sharper than any double-edged sword, it penetrates even to dividing soul and spirit, joints and marrow; it judges the thoughts and attitudes of the heart."* God's word is a powerful weapon against lies. It is living and at work. This is why it is so important to be speaking the truth of God to yourself, to others and to allow others to speak it to you. When you hear God's truth it has an effect upon you. And when you hear it enough times, your beliefs begin to be transformed. You can stop believing lies. And you can start believing and living the truth.

If you need help finding verses check out the list included in the Appendix.

EXERCISE 2

Sometimes having an action to go along with learning a new truth is helpful in getting that truth to sink in. Take a large board or piece of paper and write out the lies you identified in a grid format in one or two short words. Then, write out the truth that is opposite to those lies on pieces of paper or index cards in big letters with a Bible verse that speaks to that truth written underneath. Using push pins, tape or other adhesives, cover over the lie with the truth and read the truth and its verse aloud to yourself. When you are going about your day and you realize you are believing the lie instead of the truth, go to your board, lift the card covering the lie you're struggling with and say, for example, "No, I am not worthless. I have value." Then place the card back on top of the lie and read the verse aloud that talks of your value as a child of God.

EXERCISE 3

If you have a trusted friend who you know prays for you regularly, give them a list of the lies and the truths and verses that you are trying to replace them with. Ask if they would be willing to pray through this list for you when they pray.

CHAPTER TWELVE
The Freedom of Forgiveness

It wasn't until I realized just how broken my abuse had left me that I was able to start allowing God to make me whole again. And it wasn't until that happened that my anger over what had been done to me came out in great force.

As I have shared already, I had not recognized just how profoundly my abuse had affected my life and how I lived and related with others. So I wasn't angry about it. I was ashamed and belittled, but not angry. And realizing my brokenness allowed me to become angry. Angry at what my relative had done to me. At how he had taken an innocent little girl and caused her to become a hurt and broken person. At how my life could have been so different if he had not done what he'd done. At what I'd missed out on in life and relationships. At considering the girl, teenager and young woman I could have been.

Realizing these things caused a deep sadness in me as I grieved that lost little girl. As I mourned my lost innocence and childhood. And from that sadness there came anger since I then understood just what and how much I had lost.

What had been taken from me.

I found myself raging inside.

And overwhelmed by intense feelings against my abuser. I wanted him hurt. I wanted to yell at him. To make sure he hurt as much as he had made me hurt. I thought and felt nothing kind or loving toward him in the midst of this anger.

At the same time though, I knew I could not live with this anger forever. It would only end up consuming me, destroying my life more than the abuse already had. But how do you go about getting rid of such anger over something like childhood sexual abuse?

I knew from the previous summer that it was possible to gain freedom from the pain of un-forgiveness that I thought I'd live with for the rest of my life. My current anger was intense, but I was determined to move through it with God in order to be freed from it. I wanted to live free of my anger and pain. And I also did not want to dwell so much on the person who caused me such pain and in my anger he was all I could think of.

God, in his great timing, sent a couple to speak to us about relationships. And he used them and their story to touch my angry life. We talked about all different aspects of relationships including how to deal with the deep pain that can result from some of the things people do to us. From hurtful experiences that leave their mark on us. As it turned out, both the speakers had been sexually abused. And both of them had been able to find healing. In particular, they both had been able to forgive their abusers and move on from their deep pain and anger.

Forgive their abusers? How is that possible?

Better yet, why would a person want to forgive someone who had done something so horrible to them?

I think there are a few important ideas to understand about forgiveness. It is not about saying that what a person has done is okay. It is not excusing them from their actions or words. Not saying that a relationship will be all peachy keen with them in the future, or possible at all.

Forgiveness is about letting go.

It is about acknowledging that we do not want to continue living with the pain and anger anymore and giving that up to God. It is about giving God the job of dealing with that person that hurt us so much. It is about finding peace and grace in the midst of our lives. It is about dealing with that which we have control of: our actions, our thoughts and our lives. Forgiveness is about being freed to live the life we were created to live, unhindered by the pain and lies of the words and actions of others.

At the same time that I was considering these ideas of forgiveness I was also thinking about a few things in regard to my abuser. Abuse usually does not happen in a vacuum. There is a reason a person sexually abuses another and as I thought about my abuser and what I knew about him I realized that he had most likely been abused himself. He was fairly young and in a place of trying to figure out who he was, and perhaps what had been done to him. Having this perspective of him caused my feelings for him to soften. I was not excusing what he had done to me, but I had the understanding that he was operating out of the pain and brokenness of sexual abuse himself.

And the conversation I had had with my mom about how my abuser had become a Christian was in my thoughts as well. As I shared already, I knew that when he had accepted Jesus' forgiveness for his sins that he had been made whole and free from his own sin and brokenness.

While I was still struggling with a lot of anger toward him, these realizations helped move me toward what inevitably had to happen in my life: forgiving my abuser.

Toward the end of the week that this couple was with us, talking with us about relationships, they led an evening of prayer and ministry specifically geared to help us all find release, freedom and forgiveness in the areas we each needed it. All the tables and chairs were cleared from the center of the lecture room we met in and a fire was built in the fireplace. We were given paper and pens to write what we needed to say to any person who had hurt us. Who we needed to forgive. Any relationship we needed to let go of. And then we were given time to write and pray and to offer our writing up to God by burning our paper in the fire. Burning our thoughts and words as a symbol of what we were doing before God: giving our hurt, anger, pain and whatever else to God and asking to be freed from it.

It was an act of letting go.

I knew I had to do this. To give all my anger and hurt up to God. To let go of my anger toward my abuser.

And it was so difficult.

I sat on the floor of that room for a long time without doing a thing. There was a battle going on in my head and my heart. I knew I had to write my feelings out on paper. I had to address them to my abuser, telling him that what he did to me was horrible. That it messed up my life and caused me a lot of pain. That my life could have been different if he had not abused me. That I was angry at him. But it took me a long time to actually begin writing.

As I think back on that evening I can still feel the struggle that went on within me. I wanted my hand to start writing, but something was keeping it from doing so. I would pick up the pen and put it above the paper and sit there, only to throw the pen down again unable to follow through. I did this several times before anything was written. I know God was with me in those intense moments and I know it was him who gave me the grace to start writing. Because once I did it all flowed out. I told my abuser exactly what I was thinking and feeling. I told him of my anger, my pain. I told him that he had taken my life away from me. That I was not the person I could have been because of him.

I got it all out on paper and sat back knowing a tremendous relief!

It was so good to get it out of me. In a way I think I was purging my body of all that anger and pain because it has never come back.

Then I took my piece of paper, brought it up to the fire, and with tears streaming down my face I put that paper in the fire and asked God to remove the pain and anger from me. I told him that I forgave my abuser for what he had done to me. That I wanted to live in the freedom and wholeness that was available to me through Jesus. It was an intense moment in my life. But it brought about such an amazing change in who I was and how I lived.

I felt set free and full of life.

I was renewed and filled with joy!

I am so glad I was given that opportunity that evening. It was my chance to confront my abuser in the only way I could since he had died years ago. It was also a way for me to put closure on my anger and pain. I really did walk away from that evening a new person.

A freed person.

A person at peace with life.

And I can look back on it and recognize that evening as a turning point and the beginning of a whole new path in life. It stands like a signpost on a road that tells me what lay in the past and what is in the future.

Because of that night I am no longer the victim of abuse, but a new creation set free to live a joyful and abundant life!

Praise God!

Chapter Twelve:
Personal Application

EXERCISE 1

Spend time thinking over your life. Are there people you need to forgive? Are there big things, or little things, that you are holding on to with unforgiveness? Ask God to show you how that lack of forgiveness has a hold on you. And ask him to help you get to the place where you are ready to forgive. To let go of the hurt and pain and move forward with your life. Consider writing your own letters to express your anger and hurt and then burn them in your own fire. It is a tangible act of letting go of those things that have a hold on you.

EXERCISE 2

Meditate on the following verses on forgiveness. What do you hear God saying to you through them?

> Matthew 6:14 — *"For if you forgive men when they sin against you, your Heavenly Father will also forgive you."*

> Luke 23:34a — *"Jesus said, 'Father, forgive them, for they do not know what they are doing,'"* (what he said about those who killed him).

> Colossians 3:13 — *"Bear with each other and forgive whatever grievances you may have against one another. Forgive as The Lord forgave you."*

Colossians 4:32 — *"Be kind and compassionate to one another, forgiving each other, just as in Christ God forgave you."*

EXERCISE 3

Corrie ten Boom, a woman from Holland who helped many Jews escape the Nazis and who was herself put in a concentration camp during World War II, said, "To forgive is to set a prisoner free and to discover the prisoner was you." Think about this statement. Do you struggle with this idea, or does it ring true for you? Are you able to recognize that a lack of forgiveness does make you a prisoner? What is it about unforgiveness that holds you in bondage? Are you willing to do what it takes to become free?

CHAPTER THIRTEEN
A Box of Jewels

God gave me a wonderful confirmation that summer that a change had indeed taken place within me. Just as the image of the waves showed up in both my summers in England, there was an image of a box of jewels that God used to speak to me about my life and learning to be open to him in all things. To trust him. To allow him to grow me, to heal me, to work through me. And then telling me that I had learned to trust him, to be grown, healed and worked in.

Two times during my first summer there a fellow student named Ruth said she saw the image of a box of jewels when everyone was praying for me. It was a closed box that contained many beautiful, precious stones that God wanted to reveal. She shared that I was that box. That I had those beautiful, precious stones in me that God wanted to share with me and with the world.

But like the box, I was closed.

Tightly.

It was up to me to open the box to allow God to show me the glorious riches inside. In order for those things to touch my life, my future, the world around me.

I remember being very confused the two times she shared this picture with me. Seeing it made her cry and weep for me. She urged me to let my box be opened because then I would be free. Then God could enjoy with me the treasure within. The treasure he had put inside me.

But I didn't understand.

I thought I was "open" to what God was doing in me. The picture did not touch me like it was clearly touching Ruth as she prayed for me and shared what God was showing her about me.

Just like with the ocean waves, this was an image that would come back to me the following summer. And just like when my friend Nina told me she saw a perfectly calm ocean with no waves, someone who did not know me on my DTS, or about the unopened box of jewels, would see something in prayer that stopped me short and put a smile on my face. That second summer while helping to lead the DTS, we had a time of prayer.

While everyone was praying for me, one of our students said she saw a box.

A box full of beautiful, precious stones.

And the box was opened.

And God was showing me my precious stones, rejoicing in their beauty. Enjoying their sparkle and brilliance. I was amazed at how God spoke to me. How he let me know how I was doing.

I do not think I could have become that open box of beautiful jewels without dealing with my abuse. Without sharing about it. Without realizing its impact on my life and going through the sadness and anger that followed. And without forgiving my abuser.

Until I did these things I could not be fully open to God and to becoming who he created me to be, because until I dealt with these issues they were what defined my life. It was only afterward that I was able to really discover who Jennifer is. Who I have been created to be and what I've been created to do. To realize much more fully the gifts and talents that I have been given and to know the freedom and confidence to share them with others.

Thinking back on that summer, I know I "knew" my gifts and talents and what I was passionate about, but I can see that I was definitely being held back from fully living and sharing those things. I was closed. And the jewels that are my gifts and talents, what I have to offer the world, the beauty of who I am, these things were locked inside of me.

While I was a person defined by painful lies and brokenness I could not freely live my purpose and abilities.

It was only upon shedding those painful things, learning the truth about who I am as a woman of God, that my life began to be defined by other things. Things like meekness; laughter; a more complete love for myself, for God and for others; empathy toward other people and their pain; joy; the manifest victory of Jesus over death, sin and Satan; confidence in my freedom and new life; a strength of purpose; wisdom; a stronger faith in God and ability to trust in him in all things.

These things weren't fully learned or realized over night. But operating under this changed understanding of who I am allowed me to begin living in a whole new way.

Chapter Thirteen:
Personal Application

EXERCISE 1

Read back over your journal entries and look at any artwork you have done in the process of going through this book. Consider where you were, and who you were, at the beginning and compare that with where you are, and who you are, now. In what ways have you changed? How are you still the same? Where would you like to see more change and/or healing in your life? How have you become more of the person God has created you to be? Do you feel set free from things that once held you captive, or do you still feel bound by things?

Change, growth and healing are a process. They do not happen over night. BUT, they do happen when we open ourselves up to God and ask him to change us, to grow us and to heal us. Keep your eyes on The Lord. Keep reading his word. Keep looking for the anchors and sign posts in your life. Keep praying to him while alone and with others. Keep worshipping him. These things are vital to him being able to work in us and to us becoming more the person he wants and needs us to be in his kingdom. And keep journalling. Sometimes we forget things that happen and it is helpful and encouraging to look back on where we were six months ago, a year ago, five years ago.

EXERCISE 2

Meditate on the following verses. What encouragement do they give you? How do they give you strength to keep moving forward with your journey of life?

2 Corinthians 4:16-18 — *"Therefore we do not lose heart. Though outwardly we are wasting away, yet inwardly we are being renewed day by day. For our light and momentary troubles are achieving for us an eternal glory that far outweighs them all."*

Philippians 1:6b — *"He who began a good work in you will carry it on to completion until the day of Christ Jesus."*

Hebrews 10:19-24 — *"Therefore, brothers, since we have confidence to enter the Most Holy Place by the blood of Jesus, by a new and living way opened for us through the curtain, that is, his body, and since we have a great priest over the house of God, let us draw near to God with a sincere heart in full assurance of faith, having our hearts sprinkled to cleanse us from a guilty conscience and having our bodies washed with pure water. Let us hold unswervingly to the hope we profess, for he who promised is faithful. And let us consider how we may spur one another on towards love and good deeds."*

Hebrews 12:1-2 — *"Therefore, since we are surrounded by such a great cloud of witnesses, let us throw off everything that hinders and the sin that so easily entangles, and let us run with perseverance the race marked out for us. Let us fix our eyes on Jesus, the author and perfecter of our faith, who for the joy set before him endured the cross, scorning its shame, and sat down at the right hand of the throne of God."*

1 Peter 1:3-5 — *"Praise be to the God and Father of our Lord Jesus Christ! In his great mercy he has given us new birth into a living hope through the resurrection of Jesus Christ from the dead, and into an inheritance that can never perish, spoil or fade - kept in heaven for you, who through faith are shielded by God's power until the coming of the salvation that is ready to be revealed in the last time."*

EXERCISE 3

Spend time writing out a prayer to God. Express your thankfulness for the work he's done in you so far. Confess things that need to be given up to him. Ask him for help in the areas you need him to help you. And commit your life to him. Then, decorate it. Make is special and put it in a special place. Read it from time to time. Use this like a stone marker on the path of your life so that it stands out and gives direction.

CONCLUDING THOUGHTS

As I finish up this telling of my story I am several years removed from this life changing time. I have gone to seminary, gotten married and am now a stay-at-home mother with two precious little girls. I am so thankful for this time in my life. Time to face challenges. To grow. To heal. To become the little girl chasing pigeons. I can not imagine being the wife and mother that I am today without having gone through all these things. And not just that; I could not be the woman I am, the friend, the member of the body of Christ that I am without this healing and change.

Like I said in the beginning, this story of mine is not really my own. It is every woman's story. We all have hurts, disappointments, people who squelch our zeal for life. We all have hopes and dreams and visions for who we want to be. We all have confusion and misunderstandings. We all feel trapped by events, feelings, people, situations, and maybe by things we can't even put a name to.

And we were all created to be more than someone held captive by sin, hurt and disappointment.

We were made to be free!

To live fully. To be washed clean and made new.

We were made to be vessels of our living God in this world for his glory. We've been given gifts and talents and God wants to use them to bring change and healing in the lives of others.

Sometimes I watch my little girls running around, giggling, singing, creating worlds of their imagining. So carefree and innocent. So trusting and full of life. So secure in the love my husband and I have for them. That is what we are to be like when we have God as our Heavenly Father. He can take all our brokenness, all our sin, all our pain, all our distrust and make us new. New to run and live and laugh in the joy of his abundant life.

It is my prayer that everyone who reads this story will find their way to becoming that free and joyful little girl.

Go chase pigeons!

APPENDIX

The following list of verses is taken from a list in Neil T. Anderson's book The Bondage Breaker that show us who we are, and what we have, as Children of God.

John 1:12 — I am a child of God.
John 15:6 — I have been chosen to be fruitful.
Romans 5:1 — I am justified.
Romans 8:1-2 — I am free from condemnation.
Romans 8:35-39 — I am secure.
1 Corinthians 3:16 — I am God's temple.
1 Corinthians 6:17 — I am united with the Lord and one with Him in spirit.
1 Corinthians 6:20 — I have been bought with a price and belong to God.
Ephesians 2:10 — I am God's workmanship.
Ephesians 2:18 — I have direct access to God through his Holy Spirit.
Ephesians 3:12 — I am welcome to approach God.
Philippians 3:20 — I am a citizen of heaven.
Philippians 4:13 — I am capable.
Colossians 1:14 — I have been redeemed and forgiven of all my sins.
Colossians 2:10 — I am complete.
1 John 5:18 — I am born of God and Satan cannot touch me.

I'm including a list of books I've read in the course of my healing and growing process. I hope they are helpful to you and your own journey in life.

- To Be Told: Know Your Story Shape Your Future (and workbook) by Dan B. Allender
- The Wounded Heart: Hope For Adult Victims of Childhood Sexual Abuse (and workbook) by Dr. Dan B. Allender
- The Bondage Breaker by Neil T. Anderson
- Unleashing God's Power In You by Neil T. Anderson and Robert L. Saucy
- Victory Over the Darkness: Realizing the Power of Your Identity in Christ by Neil T. Anderson
- Boundaries by Dr. Henry Cloud and Dr. John Townsend
- Changes That Heal: How to Understand Your Past to Ensure a Healthier Future by Dr. Henry Cloud
- Inside Out by Dr. Larry Crabb
- SoulTalk: The Language God Longs For Us to Speak by Larry Crabb
- Captivating: Unveiling the Mystery of a Woman's Soul by John Eldredge and Stasi Eldredge
- The Dance of Life: Weaving Sorrows and Blessings into One Joyful Step by Henri J.M. Nouwen
- Hope For the Flowers by Trina Paulus
- Disappointment With God by Philip Yancey

ABOUT THE AUTHOR

Jennifer Mahnke is a wife, mother of two, quilter, Anglican, bookworm, CrossFitter, and co-owner of a baby accessory business called Crafty Pants. Her ultimate passion though is to see women's lives transformed from brokenness to abundant freedom and joy. She juggles all these interests and passions on the North Shore of Boston, Massachusetts.

Made in the USA
Middletown, DE
03 December 2022

16813235R00070